Soccer Brain:
The 4C Coaching Model for Developing World Class Player Mindsets and a Winning Football Team

by Dan Abrahams

BENNION
KEARNY

Published in 2013 by Bennion Kearny Limited.

ISBN: 978-1-909125-04-9

Published by Bennion Kearny Limited
6 Victory House
64 Trafalgar Road
Birmingham
B13 8BU

www.BennionKearny.com

Cover image: ©Shutterstock/Krivosheev Vitaly

To Heidi and to Zoe

"Every great dream begins with a dreamer. Always remember, you have within you the strength, the patience, and the passion to reach for the stars to change the world"
Harriet Tubman

Acknowledgements

I'd firstly, and most importantly, like to thank my wife Heidi. You are, to quote a famous poet, my north, my south, my east and west (and a little more besides). Thanks for being there, for supporting and for editing (it takes a certain skill to edit a book about soccer when it's far from being your favourite subject area).

A big thanks to James, my publisher, without whom there would be no book to thank anyone for in the first place. Your wisdom is much appreciated.

Finally, a big thanks to Wayne Burnett who got the ball rolling, to Steve Gallen for continuing the momentum, and to all the coaches and managers I've worked with over the years.

About the Author

Dan Abrahams is a freelance sport psychologist who specialises in soccer. He has spent the past decade working with some of the leading soccer players, teams, organisations and governing bodies globally. He has held contracts with leading clubs in the English Premier League and some of the top managers and coaches regularly use his techniques to drive their coaching culture and team building processes.

Dan's passion is to de-mystify sport psychology and deliver simple and practical ideas to both players and coaches. He is a regular speaker at soccer conferences across Europe wowing audiences with his engaging, upbeat, positive and fun presentations and workshops.

Dan has spread his soccer psychology philosophies across the soccer globe by using social media and his mindset techniques are now used by players and coaches across Europe, the USA, the Middle East, the Far East and Australasia.

Table of Contents

Introduction
The Toughest Profession of All

You are the coach. You are the leader. You are responsible.

You stand in front of them, their eyes transfixed on you, their minds set for your instruction. A match of significance, of high stakes. A win and your position is safe, a loss and the exit door looms.

Your words will travel with them into this game – what you say has to have impact. You can see they are nervous, as are you. But you can't show them that – heart rate steady, stay composed, a still rational mind is best.

Pre match simplicity: nothing new now, just reinforcement. Start with a soft voice then raise the tone – now lessen the volume as the room intensity sizzles. Calm minds are a must, no headless chickens.

Their roles and responsibilities: emphasize. Emotional words for some, words of action for others. Then togetherness, that invisible rope that binds us. A focus on the team – just about us, what *we* do, not what *they* do.

Memory – replace fear with confidence using reminders of past successes against this team. An emphatic win and a hard fought draw. Every second counts if they're going to repeat those outcomes – every second of grind, of freedom, of focus.

Time! No more talking – so easy to say too much. Now positive action. The tunnel, then pitch, then technical area. A little instruction from the sidelines maybe, but they are on their own now. Let them fly!

Soccer Brain

You, however, are *not* on your own. A coach is never truly isolated. You have resources to be the very best you can be, and I'd like you to come out of your comfort zone and stretch yourself. I'd like you to engage in the improvement process.

I'd like you spend every day, every coaching session, and every minute of training and match day becoming the best coach you can be.

This book will help you do that. It will help you monitor your thoughts, philosophies, values, systems, actions and behaviours as you go about your daily coaching practices. It will challenge and stretch you. It will require you to question the methodologies and coaching beliefs that you may hold dear. It will, of course, also reinforce – I'm sure you have some winning habits that you already employ on your eager students. I hope *Soccer Brain* will help you magnify your strengths as a coach but also tease a few extra ideas out of the pedagogical system you use now.

My passion is the extension of soccer talent; to help footballers improve and perform. Young, veteran, working class, middle class, boy or girl, every race, colour and creed - my life is spent helping shape the performances of those who play the beautiful game. Making them pitch perfect is my driving creed. Do you share this obsession? Do you wake up excited about the training session you're going to put on that afternoon or night? Do you go to bed wondering how you could have done the sessions that little bit better? Does your mind vibrate when you ask yourself how you can accelerate the learning of a few more of your players? If you feel this way, if you have that ardent fervour, that zeal to help footballers then you *are* the right person to read *Soccer Brain*.

As much as I love helping footballers, my obsession extends to coaching. Working alongside great soccer coaches makes me excited. It helps me understand not only soccer but also the subtle nuances of learning and performance. Listening to a great coach in action on the training ground is (to me) akin to listening to great poets read their verse. What do I hear? I hear the complex made simple, the reinforcement of correct action, the right questions asked, the silence that 'says a thousand words', the emotion appropriately apportioned, and the use of language that inspires and aspires. Off the pitch I see many things – I see meticulous detail in planning, I see preparation for all eventualities, I see collaboration with players, I see a winning culture driving player adherence, and I see excitement in the face of evolving club objectives. And both on and off the pitch I sense – I sense the notion of fun, freedom and focus, I sense personal guidance and professional leadership, I sense openness and caring, I sense a will to win but also a commitment to learn, and I sense failure as a resource for success.

Mindset and Coaching Culture

Be warned, this isn't a traditional soccer coaching book. There will be no sketches of drills and plays. There is no real talk of formation, or shape and pattern. When you scan a page you won't find bullet points fine-detailing the art of controlling a football or where to place players for a corner kick. These are the technical and tactical sides of the game that are your traditional sources of information as a coach. They are detailed in plenty of resources elsewhere.

With this book, however, your ability to instruct the tactical and technical components of the game will improve and your players' skill in executing your tuition will develop if you build its messages into your coaching. This is because this book is intended to drive your mindset as a coach, the mentality of your players and the culture of your coaching practice. Great coaching, a player's ability to understand and learn, and a player's expression of bodily movement in performance starts with these qualities.

To me mindset and culture are analogous to the importance of soil and water to a plant. A plant won't grow and bloom the most beautiful flowers if you don't use the right soil type and if you fail to water it on a regular basis. Similarly, your players won't develop and perform if you don't have the right coaching culture in place and the right strategies to develop both your mindset and the mindset of your players.

Mindset and coaching culture are the hidden mediators of success as a coach. They are the silent determinants of improvement and development. To me if there is such a thing as 'the secret' of coaching it is 'Mindset and Coaching Culture'.

A Little Self-Awareness

Take a step back from your coaching practice for a moment and exercise your self-awareness:

- What is your mindset as a coach like?
- What is your ability to change the mindset of your players like?
- What is your coaching culture like?

These are three of the most important questions you can ask yourself as a coach. Three questions holding answers that separate the very best from the rest, and three questions whose answers form the continuum of being a winning coach. To me, failure in a coaching role is more often than not related to your failure to deliver on one or more of these areas.

I want you to start thinking and answering these questions *now*; in this book we are going to work hard to develop these three components of coaching.

Technique and Tactics aren't the only things in the playbook

Allow me to strong arm you here. Do you think because you know about systems, shape and patterns of play (maybe all of them in the play book) that you are a great coach? Do you think because you have a folder full of drills for every specific situation encountered on the pitch you are an accomplished coach?

Note: I recently worked at a professional football club where a coach proudly showed me a crammed folder full of drills. He was the same coach who refused to inform one of his senior players that he wouldn't be playing the following week and failed to give the player an explanation why. He immediately lost the trust and confidence of that player. Who cares about his folder full of drills!?!

Technique and tactics aren't the only things in the coach's playbook! I cannot deny that they are your fundamentals. A coach without a sound knowledge of these elements of the game is not a coach at all. But 'knowing' is not 'doing' especially when the 'doing' part is an art and not an exact science. In coaching it is the brush strokes that mediate success not the palette itself.

Tactical genius only travels so far. Knowing what changes to make at any given moment during a game is a must-have skill, but if the management of mindsets and the development of a coaching culture conducive to excellence is beyond the coach then the tactics board will have less impact. Likewise an eye for developing technical wizardry helps build the modern player machine but helping footballers combine the technical skills to cope with the tightest and toughest of plays requires player buy-in and group confidence.

Quite simply the coaching of technique and tactics in football are built on a foundation of mindset and culture. Let me explain. Coaches adhering to these philosophies deliver students of the game – they are enablers of a great learning mentality. Similarly, player competence is underpinned by individual confidence – a mental quality that coaches drive through patience, repetition, reinforcement, re-appraisal and relationship. Furthermore, coaches who apply techniques to develop player focus and distraction management help players perform under pressure.

The coach who points to the poor positioning of a centre back as blame for a conceded goal would benefit from examining the 'internal' that delivers the 'external'. It might be that the centre back *knows* where to position herself – it was just a moment of distraction that found her in the wrong place at the wrong time. Similarly, the coach who faces her players at the end of a tough defeat may thunder about the ease with which the team's shape had broken down. But perhaps she should exercise her thinking about *her players' thinking* instead. Team shape follows thought, confidence and understanding – soft skills mediating the hard skills. Indeed, there are so many reasons why teams may win or lose – tactics aren't the whole story of coaching. They never have been and they never will be.

Likewise, if you are a coach of younger players - a time when working on technique is crucial - then mindset and coaching culture are important determinants of skill acquisition. Just because you tell them what to do, and show them what to do, doesn't mean they will easily be able to do it. And just because they can't do it the first, second or third time doesn't mean they can't be good at the game. Talent comes in many forms and your coaching culture and ability to develop mindset can tap a player's development sweet spot. Technique is heavily mediated by mindset – always has been and always will be.

To my mind the path to coaching excellence lies in this simple equation - brain first, body second. This may be a slightly different viewpoint to yours so allow me to elaborate. Technique and tactics reside in your brain, not in your feet or your legs or your heart. Technique and tactics are scripted, encrypted and executed in the wiring that sits behind the eyes – the wiring that delivers the message that the body follows. Once a coach understands this he gives himself permission to set himself apart from his peers.

Player Mindset

You will set yourself apart if you get to grips with the concept that coaching starts with the mindset of the player. Allow me to say that again because it is an important point for you to reflect on – coaching starts with the mindset of the player.

Coaching starts with your ability to captivate, to enthral, to interest, and to attend to the individual need.

Coaching starts with player belief and confidence and certainty.

Coaching starts with your ability to focus minds, to shift attention, to manage emotion.

Coaching starts with a player's needs and wants and doubts and hopes and dreams and fears and values.

Coaching starts with "Where can I take this player" and "Where can I take this team" and "Where can I take this club".

Coaching requires ownership of the player experience. Not just through drill or through exercise – these play a part but they don't produce champions. Champion soccer players find their way to the top of the pile through the people skills they have been exposed to along their journey.

The Toughest of Professions

I believe coaching is one of the toughest professions (or hobbies) you can undertake.

My reasoning lies in the fact that as a coach you deal with human beings – specifically human learning and performance. In other words you deal in chaos –

a clashing of a collection of brains, minds and bodies that individually and collectively function more powerfully than the highest spec computers.

With your squad of players in front of you (and some of you can throw your backroom support staff into this mix) you are dealing with the values, experiences, needs, wants, beliefs, fears, and desires that drive and underpin the complex behaviours you see in and around the training ground and on match day. It matters little what age group you coach, the landscape is endlessly complex and your functioning as a coach is constantly stretched. The twists and turns a season takes is startling and your emotional compass will shift constantly as one challenge fuses into the next.

I don't say this to strike a negative chord with you – more to extend my arm and shake you by the hand for choosing a worthwhile endeavour. And I think (and hope) I have something that can help you.

My 4C Model

Of the many thousands of hours I've spent with both players and coaches I've noticed key patterns develop. I've learnt what players want and how coaches can give it to them. I've learnt what coaches do when they are at their best and what they don't do when things don't go according to plan.

Whilst the odd tactical mistake can happen it is primarily mindset and coaching culture that, in my experience, sparks great games, champagne moments, breakthrough teams and winning streaks. It is mindset and coaching that can, conversely, generate poor performances, nightmare matches, tough breaks and losing runs.

Great coaching isn't always tangible. It's quite often invisible. There are no hard and fast rules – it's an art not an exact science. But over the years I have found that, when it comes to mindset and coaching culture, you have to tick certain boxes to be a winning coach. The system I have developed to do this is the *4C Coaching Model*.

The 4C Coaching Model

When I use the word culture what exactly do I mean? What exactly is culture?

It is *what you say* and *what you do* and *how you say it* and *how you do it*. It relates to behaviours, attitudes, habits and norms. It refers to perception, thinking and feeling. It provides identity and satisfaction.

Just as customer service, revenue and profit are heavily influenced by organisational culture in the business world, so your players' and team's ability to develop technically, execute tactically and manage mentally are effected by your coaching culture.

It can be teasingly simple yet enduringly complex to get right. You can develop an outstanding culture yet you can't have a perfect one. Let's have a brief look at the 4C's within the Coaching Model before we get started.

A Culture of Creativity

You the coach must have the capacity to trigger a culture of creativity.

Your coaching culture should avoid the sterile. It should embrace change at the right time. It should seek improvement in all areas as the season progresses. There should be no standing still. Creative solutions are required to increase team victories and aid player improvement. Getting stuck in tired coaching solutions won't help you build the team of the 21st century nor develop the players of the future.

You must seek no stone left unturned to learn all you can. You must leverage old information and decorate it with new science. You must nurture players through the reinvention of knowledge from yesteryear. You must cultivate through insight, support through innovation, and put your own spin on the practices of the master coaches.

The coach who asks questions of current procedures and methodologies and immerses herself in finding new solutions will win out. She will advance quicker than her rivals. The coach who refuses to stand still and refuses to accept common practice in favour of more radical training protocols will be rewarded. Boldness is the best friend of the future soccer coach.

The first section of Soccer Brain takes a broad brush approach to helping you improve your culture of creativity. You will be asked to accelerate your learning and development as a teacher. You will be introduced to a different definition of talent – one that will open your eyes to possibility. And you will be invited to explore the small things that can have a big impact on your coaching outcomes.

A Confident Culture

You, the coach, must have the capacity to trigger a Culture of Confidence.

How? You must believe in yourself and in your coaching methodologies. You must believe in every decision you take and every plan you create. And alongside this you must believe with all your heart that your players can become anything they want to be. You must believe the unthinkable, *the impossible*. You must be the optimist (perhaps the mindless optimist at times). You must believe with all your heart that you can make a great soccer player out of anyone who turns up for a trial or practice match. You must believe in your team as a group of winners even when they lose, even when they lie exhausted on the floor beaten from the first minute to the last.

Your culture of confidence starts with your mindset, for your mindset not only transfers to your players but also resonates throughout your club, your squad and your organisation. But this doesn't mean you are blind to what you need to improve (as is discussed in sections one and three). Being truly confident in any domain requires a close inspection of what needs to go better. Excellence is enveloped by past failures and sealed by learning from defeat. Optimism, yes – ignorance, no!

For many (and I agree with this notion) it is belief that separates the best from the also-rans. It is belief that governs potential, and belief that ultimately determines success. When you watch a champion in any sport there is more than hard work at play. There is a certainty, an all knowing absorption of belief in self that drives world class technique and tactics and ultimately world class performance. You, the coach, must contribute to this – for every word you say, every sentence your players hear impacts upon their focus, their learning, their self-belief and subsequently their performance confidence.

Section two of Soccer Brain will give you the philosophies and the mindset tools to deliver a Culture of Confidence. You will be given the ingredients to create an environment conducive to building self-belief in your players. Your coaching tool kit will expand with a series of belief developing techniques. You will be able to use these on yourself to encourage your own self-belief. And finally section two will introduce you to training protocols that help enhance your team's performance confidence.

A Committed Culture

You, the coach, must have the capacity to trigger a Committed Culture.

The champion commits under pressure. She doesn't lurch from one bad thought to the next. She doesn't allow herself to become engulfed in emotion as she competes. She doesn't snap out of her high performance mindset just because she's gone a goal down.

Do you have players who know what to do in the heat of battle when adversity strikes? Do you have a simple system for them to snap into the right mindset before they play? Are they routine driven on match day?

The champion commits to being the very best she can be. She is passionate about training to improve, not just training for the sake of it or because she is required to. The champion is engrossed in practice. The champion loves nothing better than to stretch her comfort zone – she dares to take a backward step, to look stupid in practice so her skills improve at a relentless pace.

Do you have players who will work in training for you, for themselves and for their teammates? Are they goal oriented? Are they dedicated to the cause of self-improvement and performance? Do they go into training hoping they are going to improve or do they venture onto the practice field *knowing* they will improve? Do they have a formula to be the very best individual they can be?

Section three of Soccer Brain helps you weave a culture that increases player commitment on and off the field of play. You will learn how to help your players apply a mental structure as they compete. They will become the ruthless competitor. The section will also help you to improve their engagement in training. They will become better, faster learners of your drills and exercises. You will discover the science and art of intentional practice and you will learn how to squeeze every last drop of ability out of them.

A Cohesive Culture

You, the coach, must have the capacity to trigger a Cohesive Culture.

A great coach 'teams' her players. She starts with a group of individuals and gently, carefully assembles them into a team unit. She does this through her voice, through her actions and her behaviours.

In the words of the great Michael Jordan "Talent and intelligence wins games but teamwork wins championships." Picture Barcelona. Picture Bayern Munich. Picture Manchester United. Great teams think together, predict together and move together. Individuals team when they see what each other see. When they know what each other knows. When they want what each other wants.

Sure, a great team is a product of shared tactical play. But a great team is also a collection of shared mindsets. A great team is a product of purposeful communication – ideally through spoken language but also through non verbal behaviour. Players of different nationalities and disparate dialects can play together cohesively by means of observation of body language, movement and action.

Section four of Soccer Brain helps you create a cohesive unit of players and people. You will learn about soccer specific leadership. I will share a model with you that I introduce to clients who coach at all levels. I will also take a slightly different stance on cohesion. Teams are a collaboration between individuals – 'we' begins with 'me', I firmly believe that. Finally, you will be introduced to the technical aspects of team building. Players that are passionate about team processes are the ones who bring home the trophies. Providing a team framework for success related to on field activities are more powerful than the social bonding that is prevalent in the team building industry.

Does Age and Level Matter?

Yes they do. It's very challenging to write a book that covers the coaching process for all ages and all levels. In fact to satisfy everyone completely is impractical. The coach of 8 year olds isn't going to deliver the same style, nor will he trade in the same game improvement philosophies as a coach instructing 18 year olds. Similarly, the coach at grassroots level will take a different approach to the coach who works at a professional club. But I hope you feel that *all* soccer coaches can learn from this book and I place the onus on you, the coach, to scaffold ideas or make them more complex where necessary.

I'd like you to see this as both a challenge and an advantage. The simple process of reading and copying will never provide you with a deep learning experience. In contrast, taking ideas, philosophies, tools and techniques and adapting them to fit into your specific coaching programme and structure will provide you with a longer lasting, deeper developmental process.

Success as a Coach

Soccer players, no matter what their age, no matter what their level, can be tough to manage. They can be demanding, unruly and inattentive. They can be inconsistent, stroppy and emotionally engulfed. Their games can fluctuate for what may appear no rhyme or reason. Soccer, the game we love, does this to people. It is frustrating and infuriating but equally uplifting and energising. It offers a melting pot of mixed emotion.

How is success as a coach done? Let me give you a few thoughts before you turn to section one.

- *Success as a coach is fuelled by habit and pattern – yours and the ones you teach away from the lights and behind the curtain. Make your habits and patterns excellent. You can never have too many of them. You can never get them good enough!*
- *Success as a coach is a result of a combination of all the mini instructions in all the sessions you conduct over time. There is never a throw away remark or a casual drill. All sentences uttered, all drills executed, count. They add up to build or to break. Choose your words and your behaviours carefully!*
- *Success is a product of the intangibles – the stuff your players don't notice. It's under the behavioural surface that so often counts. It's away from the lights of match day where the hard coaching work is done. It's the quality of your sessions that creates champions. Note the intangibles every day and in every session.*

- *Success as a coach is decided by the six inches between the ears – yours and theirs - more so than in the feet or in the body. Success as a coach is decided by your ability to turn a vision into reality – it's about changing the world for your players and your team. Success as a coach is decided by more than technical ability or tactical mastery. It's decided by the Soccer Brain – yours and theirs.*

Two things about Soccer Brain… just so you know.

1. In this book, I will interchangeably use the terms soccer and football, as well as soccer player and footballer.

2. Included in the text are some of the Tweets I post every day on the Twitter website that aim to get soccer players, coaches and fans debating the performance mindset. I hope they are thought provoking.

Section One
A Culture of Creativity

You, the coach, must build a culture of creativity to develop your players and shape your team. Creativity finds solutions through insight, leading to novel ideas that nurture player mindset, technique and game intelligence. The coach cannot simply sit and wait for the thunderbolt of creativity. It must be gently encouraged by education. The processes of learning, absorbing, thinking, and delivering must become the four step procedure for creative coaching.

As a coach you must develop your creativity by looking under every stone and around every corner. Your base knowledge is your get go for creative ability.

Creativity is the training ground must have. It's Mourinho, it's Ferguson, it's Wenger – it follows the greats onto the practice pitch. It helps drive their thinking as they look upon their team. Their tactics are shaped by it with pattern, movement and team structure forming the heartbeat of their footballing smarts. To be like them - an innovator – the coach must share their passion and relentless search for the things other coaches haven't dared to imagine.

As a coach who likes to win - creativity must be the driving force behind your team plays. Creativity can develop robustness of defence and flexibility of attack.

The creative coach must ease back the tunnel vision that plagues so many coaches. The obvious way, the comfortable way is not for the creative coach. Nor is their mind filled with the voice of doubt – that self-censorship that holds back the creative spirit and maintains the mundane, the acceptable, and the everyday.

As a coach you must have the courage of your convictions to add or generate something new. You must squash that inner voice that whispers "You can't do it this way, you can't do it that way." You must think, as a coach, with freedom, not with fear.

This opening section to Soccer Brain introduces you to a blueprint that holds the key to implementing a culture of creativity. The formula for a culture of confidence is made up of 7 simple steps:

1. A relentless dedication to increasing knowledge
2. Being a no limit coach – qualifications are only your entry point into the profession
3. Breaking the game down into its constituent components and building knowledge in each area
4. Looking outside soccer for vital clues in the development of coaching excellence
5. Expanding your definition of talent – there is such a thing as 'mindset talent'
6. Knowing the talents in front of you
7. Being a 1%er

So, now that we know these seven steps – let's start exploring them!

1

The Roots of Creativity

'The Wizard' glared at his players. This was first practice, he knew what to say:

"I'm not going to like you all the same. You won't like me or each other all the same either. Nor will I treat you all the same."

At first glance this was an obvious opener. 'The Wizard' had a mixed set of players – two black, two white, one from a Jewish background – a diverse, All American camp who *had* to become a team. But these words arrived from experience. This was October 1963 and he had been head coach of the UCLA Bruins basketball programme since 1948. His self-development was in full flow and it was time for moderate success to grow.

Certain barriers existed. 'The Wizard' lacked magical facilities. A leggy three flights of stairs to a small and squalid gym was hardly inspiring. The practice area itself was more gymnastics than basketball with chalk from the pommel horse having to be mopped up or brushed aside before training.

But 'The Wizard', also known as Coach John Wooden, was too engrossed to notice the neglected provisions. He had a team to shape, to mould, and to introduce to excellence. As a set of individuals they weren't fancied. None of them were over 6 foot 5 inches - short in a game of height. But, as it turns out, the opening practice session scheduled in October 1963 saw him take a first glance at what was to be his 'Potential Team' – the set of players who would come as close to reaching their maximum ability as they possibly could.

It proved an emphatic year. Five times during the season his team scored more than 100 points. Only four times did the opposition stay within 5 of them. They went undefeated and won the first NCAA Championship under Coach Wooden's tenure. This was the first of many (ten in total between 1964 and 1975), but it was the first that was the sweetest for him - sweet because 'Wizard' John Wooden grew this team's potential out of his own growth.

Being John Wooden

Even *he* would have admitted that the man voted as the greatest American sports coach of all time wasn't born that way. He didn't arrive into this world as a leader of sport. It was self-learning that made him the teacher he became. It was the adversity he endured in the early years that helped him design a robust coaching system that eventually led his teams to greatness. It was a commitment to improve his communication that helped him engage those who were over 30 years his junior. It was his insistence on excellence that honed a creative mindset. It was John Wooden's devotion to self development as a coach that eventually won him Championships, plaudits, and a place in the coaching Hall of Fame.

Your culture of creativity starts with your dedication to knowing it all. You'll never get there – but those coaches who make the furthest journeys will be the best, most creative coaches they can be. It's a passage the greatest teachers take – a rocky road, a bumpy ride, but one you must take to get the very best from your players. As you progress on this voyage, your ability to think of new strategies to help your players use the talent they have will blossom. To me creativity is mediated by knowledge. Without knowledge you cannot create.

Initially Coach Wooden was cautious about transformation. I think most people are – change is the enemy of comfort. It exacts a full look at your inadequacies.

Wooden trusted his way. He was stubborn. But as Championship success eluded his beloved Bruins he steadily became more and more open to change. He took some radical steps - he attended psychology classes on campus to improve his inter- and intra-personal skills. He decided to avoid assistants who could be perceived as 'yes-men' – he wanted a loyal but challenging voice close by. He occasionally risked conflict with his players just so he could learn from the experience, and he would invite other coaches to scout his games and listen with an open mind to their comments and corrections. He spent quite a few years outside the comfort zone of his original coaching philosophies.

It matters little who you are, where you are, where you coach or who you coach. If you want to develop a culture of creativity in your club, with your team, in your soccer organisation, or at the soccer academy you work at - you *need* to have knowledge beyond the fundamentals. You need to beg for information and borrow information. You need to observe others, then expand your systems, develop new ideas, induct them into your current processes and execute when appropriate. You then need to analyse assess and evaluate what works and what doesn't. And you need to keep this course of action going for the remainder of your coaching days. Stepping beyond the ordinary drives the extraordinary in any domain.

Developing yourself as a coach makes it easier to develop those who are most important – your players

Qualifications are *Not* the Only Fruit

If Coach Wooden was a soccer coach starting out in today's coaching climate I doubt he would simply strive to pass his coaching licences, then sit back and enjoy the qualifications that adorn his office wall. On the contrary, I think he would attempt to drive his future by continually cutting into new information and shaping an ever expanding tree of knowledge.

Similarly, Coach Wooden wouldn't only borrow from the past. He didn't fashion one of the most emphatic and 'winningest' records in all of American sport by pining and yearning for the coaching methodologies of yesteryear. No doubt Wooden respected the philosophies, techniques and plays from his own time as a player, and no doubt he utilised most of them in his day to day teaching. But he also had a method of continuous improvement through research and practice.

Qualifications, licensing and certification are the entry doors you open as you step into a maze of corridors and hallways. They are not your finishing point. The UEFA A course, the UEFA Professional Licence (currently the highest coaching award in world football) and their global equivalents are your admission gates to an education as a soccer coach.

Modern day football demands life-long learning. The soccer coach is no longer a baby sitter or a drill instructor. The game challenges coaches to keep up with contemporary methodologies, sport science and talent development. I love the fact that Jose Mourinho has a degree in sport science! He has shaped some of the coaching concepts he currently uses at Spanish giants Real Madrid from the modules he studied at University. I love the fact that current Nottingham Forest manager Billy Davies has a video analysis studio built into his home in Scotland! It's his games room – his version of a child's dream space. I love the fact that Sam Allardyce, manager of West Ham in the 2012/13 season has a lifelong commitment to sport science! Everywhere Sam has coached he has utilised a sport psychologist to help improve his team's chances of winning. I love the coaches who dedicate themselves to leaving no stone left unturned in order to develop themselves and cultivate a creative culture at their club.

Never limit yourself. The coaches I've mentioned above don't. John Wooden never did. The paper that documents your qualification is not your coaching process nor is it your coaching mind. It is not your coaching life. Learning is imperative – not just from the coaches of the past but also from cutting edge research. What is coaching impossible today will become coaching possible tomorrow. Let's look a little closer at the 'so called impossible'.

Impossible Improvement for the Impossible

Allow your mind to rest on what you may perceive as the impossible within your role as a coach. Start to make a permanent internal sketch of this play. The scene should involve the impossible for you and for your players. Make it unrealistic – a flight of fantasy.

Perhaps the inner representations of this outer world features a confident, dominant and bold depiction of you standing in the technical area in the Nou Camp, Barcelona (an unlikely scenario for 99% of coaches but who cares, we're interested in the *process* of getting there - whether we do or don't).

Alternatively, perhaps the highlight reel you have envisioned centres on a scene of local players competing with fun and freedom – your instruction sparse but pertinent, your voice loud and encouraging. Whatever the inner map you have for yourself, as a coach, a central thesis of this book is to drive you to be the best you can be, and the exploration of the impossible is a part of that process – for you and your players.

I use the word impossible without embarrassment. To explore how good you can help your players become entails a look at the unlikely. There can be no limitation, restraint or constraint. For them to be their very best *you* must be your very best.

I'd like you to take some time to examine the picture you hold in your mind of the impossible. Make that picture big and bold and bright. Where are you in this image and what are you doing? How are you holding yourself? What are you saying? How do others see you? What areas of expertise do you have?

Take a pen and paper and list those areas now. Try to cover the whole page with topics – some obviously related to your field of coaching, others that might appear less relevant at first. Stretch your mind. This is your chance to note down your coaching future and the components that will create that future.

My coaching future lies in working with Under 12 – Under 14 soccer players. I want to excel at this. What does this look like? I care about them all. I take time every training session to help them individually as much as I can. I make sure I have notes on each individual at every training session – I want my communication to be as personal as is possible in group practice. I am loud and clear in my instruction but I will know when to keep quiet. I will get as perfect as I can at balancing instruction and questioning. I want to develop self-learners. I will be enthusiastic and passionate at all times – even after a poor day in the office. If I want to create passionate learners I have to be passionate myself.

This is a segment from a diary entry of a coach I work with. Success to him isn't the dizzy heights of Barcelona. But his coaching future is an exciting one. He wants to become a specialist in preparing 12-14 year olds for adult football. He knows that not all of his players are going to be soccer legends. In fact he hopes that maybe one or two of his players will go on to kick a ball for money, but that's not his primary motivation. He just wants to be the very best soccer coach he can be so he helps his young players be the very best they can be. He doesn't want to be average.

A relentless obsession to improve should be the norm
for the ambitious coach

Chapter 1

Better Than Average

Avoid average. In the decade I've worked as a specialist in football psychology I've seen too many coaches who allow 'average' to intervene. They know how to put on a decent passing drill but they don't know how to communicate in a manner conducive to building and maintaining team cohesion. They only know a *few* ways to teach a player how to increase awareness and how to exploit the space that is so often left wide open by a defence – they need to know more ways.

Likewise, they know the art of setting a team's shape but they don't know the importance of reinforcement in the teaching process so they leave too much to chance. They place too much emphasis on the role the student has in the learning process. They blame the student for not taking the information onboard.

This simply isn't good enough. Coaching is important. You as a coach are important. You affect lives beyond your own. Dreams and aspirations are reliant on your ability to problem solve, to instruct complex material in a simple manner and to develop an atmosphere conducive to learning. Taking short cuts or being too lazy to learn a subject important to your pedagogical process inhibits your coaching impact.

Being like John Wooden involves a move away from the norm. Creativity insists on novelty. Your coaching IQ increases when you open your mind to the impossible. Quite simply, within the unattainable lies clues to your coaching potential, and the capability of your players.

Not Just "Business as Usual"

Every coaching session is an opportunity to improve your players. Every minute of every hour in your coaching session provides a platform for you to impart knowledge, monitor progress, expose flaws, develop a blueprint of success and build momentum going into games. A lazy training session stifles ability. It smothers development and generates a shift away from excellence. A lazy coaching session destroys dreams.

Coaching should never be 'business as usual.' It never was for Coach Wooden. Every Wooden practice session was planned in detail to the minute. From the first whistle to the last Coach Wooden insisted on his players' best – he questioned, he queried, he told, he asked – all with the gaze and intensity of a master teacher. He knew that success was built over time - piece by piece.

Break the Game Down

I was never a footballer, but as a former professional sportsman, and professional golf coach, combined with qualifications in psychology and sport science, I've found it quite straightforward to pick up soccer from a coaching perspective – mentally, tactically and technically.

One of the disciplines that individual sports demand is the ability to break a student's game down into different components. In golf a coach is required to collapse a swing into separate mechanics – you examine the grip, stance, posture, ball position, take away, shoulder-turn, swing plane, wrist hinge, club face alignment, body weight shift, and so on. And then you break the game down further – long game, short game, putting, strategy, and mindset to name a few.

My education as a sports coach was in golf and I believe that soccer coaches would do well to copy the microscopic approach golf coaches take towards breaking a game down and building it piece by piece. A soccer coach who has techniques, philosophies and options for the minute details of the game will help his or her players develop more quickly, and win more games.

The coach who sweats the small stuff, sweats less on match day

The Game's Minutiae

What should a soccer player focus on when trying to score in order to produce optimal power and direction? Should it be the ball or should it be a specific target? Or perhaps the focus should be on an element of technique such as keeping her head over the ball? Maybe it's different for different players? For example, I worked with an English League 2 player who was on a barren run of scoring. When I asked him what he focused on as he struck the ball the player said that he tried to steer the ball into the corners of the goal. On further enquiry he was doing this because a coach had instructed him to do so - a few years previously.

As we spoke it became obvious that this was partly where his problems stemmed from. When he was a free scoring teenager he instinctively knew where the goal was – that was the easy part. At that time his focus was on the strike of the ball. He would simply exert his energy on getting a great strike on the ball and let the outcome take care of itself. The coach who came along and changed his focus had done so to the detriment of his game – his shots now lacked power and authority, and he had little confidence in, and around, the penalty box. Part of the process of improvement we worked on was for this player to get back to focusing on a great strike of the ball. He had to trust his instincts again. He knew where the goal was – that was never going to move. He had to strike the ball and let the result take care of itself.

I tell this story because I think every part of the game is coachable from shooting to tackling to physicality to mental toughness to body shape to visual awareness. And for you to be the very best coach that you can be - breaking the game down into its different components and starting to build a library of resources in relation to each area is essential. Studying the minutiae of the game is a must if you want to be the best you can be.

With this in mind let me present you with a learning challenge. Can you become the most knowledgeable coach in the world about a particular area of the game? It might be tactical, for example knowing more than anyone about playing a 442 formation. If this is your goal you might go searching for every resource dedicated to this aspect of the game. You might strive to observe great coaches who swear by its tactical potency. You might write an article on its advantages and disadvantages and offer up strategies to deal with its shortcomings. You might find someone who hates the 442 system and look to debate its merits and its failings.

Alternatively, why not try becoming a world authority on teaching players how to pass with progression?

This sounds simple doesn't it but in practice it's tough. There are a wide range of skills and knowledge pathways involved in this process. You have to be a great teacher of skill development. You have to know how to instruct players to receive a pass correctly – to be able to deaden the ball as it impacts the foot (but not so much that it gets tangled up); to collect the ball with the right body shape to be able to turn out and deliver a pass with accuracy; to strike the ball cleanly at the appropriate trajectory. From a knowledge perspective you have to know when your players should work the ball forward, and you have to be able to instruct where – does the ball go into the channels or down the middle? What should the player be seeing to decide?

You might ask yourself a few questions to drive your research on passing with progression:

What do the best passers see? What do they focus on? Do these players have anything in common? What do the best coaches do to help players become the best forward thinking passers? What drills do these coaches use to help this particular skill? How do they communicate the process to their players?

There are whole rafts of research questions to pose on every given topic in football. The competent coach resolves to search endlessly for answers. And resolution isn't always found within the soccer literature. A coach should broaden her horizons if she wants to swell her knowledge base.

It's Not Just About Soccer

To serve your players as a creative coach requires you to keep a watchful eye on theories, best practices and ideas from not only other sports, but from other disciplines in life. Personally, I find some of my most creative moments come from when I've spoken with a sports coach or participant outside of the soccer environment, or when I've read a book from the business world.

The brain has an amazing capacity to forge links between two ordinarily unrelated disciplines. There really is no limit to how good you can be as a coach if you open your mind to exploring other branches of learning and other fields of speciality.

As a coach of football your education shouldn't just revolve around football. This may sound weird or peculiar - but be assured – very few coaching breakthroughs are made when study is limited in scope. You are just as well served learning about learning, about effective forms of feedback and about the art of communication as you are about systems and formations. Novel stimuli spark the creative brain. Instead of picking up biographies that chart the life of your soccer heroes delve into books that chronicle the lives of those who have served under pressure, who have led teams in adversity, and who have made breakthroughs in the arts and sciences.

It is this attitude towards learning and knowledge – one of abundance, that allows the brain to establish a relationship, to correlate and to vibrate unconsciously and which will eventually spill ideas into conscious awareness.

This chapter is based around a central tenet of Coach John Wooden's lifetime as a coach – of basketball. His commitment to growth should be studied and modelled in the modern world of soccer. It matters little that his technical teachings lie in and revolve around a bigger ball that was bounced and was passed between hands rather than feet. It matters little that his terminologies were different, or his players were of a different physicality to a footballer. What matters is that he went about the art and science of coaching with deliberate practice and deliberate intention and his methodologies can be copied the world over to create better, stronger soccer players.

Wooden's leadership mirrors that of the greatest politicians, business people and philanthropists. They all have something to contribute to your development and your processes as a coach. As do your players.

Ridding the Muted and the Mutineers: A Confidential Audit

The biggest critics are those who are closest to you. They are at every training session, at every game, and they think about your coaching *a lot*. They are the people who either make your ideas work or damage the template you coach from. They are your players and they can offer you the greatest feedback. They can contribute to the plays you choose to move with, the style in which you coach and breadth of your encyclopaedia of coaching processes. They influence the system you choose to employ season after season.

Use them. Avoid the presence of muted players because you then end up with mutineers. Players who have no outlet for their voice or opinion end up rebelling.

Give your players a questionnaire about your coaching practices. Tell them that it's completely confidential and a tool for you to learn from and to develop your program. With this in mind it's as much for them as it is for you – they will benefit from the insights uncovered.

Ask them for honesty. You don't want personal agendas but you do want personal opinions. Provide sufficient space for explanation. If a player feels passionate that something in your training sessions isn't right they should have the opportunity to expand. If you are going to act on a suggestion you need sufficient evidence that change is required.

Strengths must be included as well as weaknesses. Any player who fails to write about their favourite part of your programme has a questionnaire that is null and void. This silently forces them to examine the strengths of your programme and helps you monitor what really works for your players. Include questions that cover all of the components that underpin your programmes. At the very least there should be enquiry into the technical, tactical, physical and mental segments of your curriculum.

A confidential audit administered is not a sign of weakness. It's an indication of coaching confidence. It sends the message that you are prepared to accept that you value the opinion of your players. It demonstrates that you understand that improvement is often hidden from a coach's view. You need that 360 degree feedback. Coaching success is laboured without it.

Your players are the bosses – so hear what the bosses have to say

An Open Mind: Scepticism not Cynicism

I pride myself with being slightly sceptical. Perhaps it's the education in psychology (a social science that tests hypotheses and demands evidence to back up its claims) that has constructed my critical mindset. I believe scepticism in a coaching role is an important quality. Believing everything that turns up on your doorstep leads to faddish coaching philosophies. Develop a robust system that can change according to the different challenges that you face, and look far and wide for new ideas to enhance your coaching structure and culture – but do so with a sceptical eye. Something new must complement and augment your existing practices or advance your system considerably for it to deserve entry into your methodology.

Scepticism is not the same as cynicism. To be cynical is to dismiss without the courtesy of evidence, experience or argument. The coach with a cynical mind deceives herself. She will miss out on ideas, forums and platforms that could take her to the next coaching level. Reject without investigation at your peril – you'll end up never knowing how good you could've been.

I receive a lot of cynicism in my career. I've been told that sport psychology doesn't work in soccer and is only applicable to individual sports. I've been declined meetings with 'the powers that be' because I don't have a first class playing career on my CV. At first such rejection bothered me, but not now. If someone refuses to offer me a stage to sell my wares I move along in the knowledge that they've missed a perfect chance to find some common ground or explore at the very least a small window of opportunity. Sceptics provide a platform, listen and ask the right questions. Cynics reject – they don't hear. Hey they don't even listen. Avoid this mindset at all costs.

Information

We live in an amazing world where information is free flowing daily. Everybody has something to learn from somebody. There are countless coaches on your doorstep for you to enquire about best coaching practices. A local coach may not have your pedigree but I can guarantee they will have some tool or technique, some story or example that you can learn from. The Spanish manager can learn from the manager of Haiti, while the manager of Manchester United can learn from the manager of a grassroots club. Ignoring those whose station in football is below yours checks your trajectory as a coach.

My passion is for you the coach to be passionate about learning. Unshackle your mind and enjoy the process of introducing processes – both old and new – into your ever evolving system. Generate new ideas. Be bold with your creativity. Try the novel in training and take to match day when appropriate. Success in coaching is a product of bravery.

Creativity is crucial especially in a coaching capacity. Your job is to get the very most from the talent you have. The creative coach is such because she takes a different view of talent. And it is this different view I want to explore now.

2
Expand your Definition of Talent

He didn't look like someone who could influence the world. Not back in August 1992.

He was your average bar hopping 30 year old. A rat race entrant who was struggling to come to terms with the normality of being ordinary. But by 2007 Time Magazine had positioned him in their Top 100 Most Influential People in the World. From zero to hero doesn't quite cut it.

His global influence had begun on a night out in '92 that was like any other guys' drinking session. Drunk and fed up, he sneaked out the back of the bar and headed home. Instead of heading to bed he did something out of the ordinary. He found an aged pair of sneakers, stripped down to his underwear and put on an old t-shirt. He then started to run.

He didn't stop. And he hasn't stopped. Since that transformative night Dean Karnazes has challenged just about every endurance running limit known to man. He has run 350 miles without sleeping. He finished second when he ran the first and only marathon to the South Pole, and at the age of 44, he completed 50 marathons in 50 consecutive days, one in each of the 50 states in America.

Despite his unparalleled running feats Karnazes doesn't believe he was born to keep on moving. As he says in his book Ultramarathon Man: Confessions of an

All-Night Runner, "I wasn't born with any innate talent. I've never been naturally gifted at anything. I always had to work at it. The only way I knew how to succeed was to try harder than anyone else. Dogged persistence is what got me through life. But here was something I was half-decent at. Being able to run great distances was the one thing I could offer the world. Others might be faster, but I could go longer. My strongest quality is that I never give up."

This is a noble passage. It encases an attitude of an optimist – "I wasn't born this way, I learnt how to do it while doing it." I admire such a sentiment and to some extent agree with its viewpoint. But let's for a moment home in on some of the words this extraordinary athlete uses - work, try harder, persistence and never give up. I think Karnazes underestimates his innate tendencies.

Karnazes IS Talented

Karnazes isn't being dishonest, but I do believe he is inadvertently bending the truth. I believe Dean Karnazes is very talented indeed. He has the talents of perseverance, of motivation, of discipline and of will and want. He puts one foot in front of the other one and continues to do so no matter what - no matter the weather, the conditions, the terrain or the distance he has run the previous day. Nothing and no-one can shake his desire to keep moving his feet forward, to keep momentum going, to stay in motion.

These are talents. These are abilities that mediate behaviours and performance and subsequently success – in sport and in life. Their existence can be found in the greatest living minds. And they are qualities that are as inborn as hand-eye coordination, mathematical ability and musical aptitude. Soft skills such as discipline, dedication and determination are gifted from birth as much as the physical skills they complement.

Of course I'm not suggesting that these virtues cannot be developed. They can, and that is one of the central messages of this chapter (and this book in fact). Every able bodied, able minded person can develop anything - be it movement, intellect or mindset. Whether they can become a 'world class performer' in these areas is another debate – but let's be clear, any competence can be improved upon.

I would guard against the notion that Dean Karnazes' soft skills aren't a part of the complex traits that people are born with. I firmly believe they are. Karnazes may or may not have an extraordinary talent to run long distances. What is unquestionable is his facility to stay motivated in the face of exhaustion – to maintain progress despite the onset of tiredness, despite blistering heat or freezing temperatures and despite excruciating physical pain. That *is* a talent he has in abundance.

Talent runs deeper than the physical. It's more than what you see on the outside

What is Sporting Talent?

Talent is universal. It lives on your street, in your neighbourhood, in your city, in your town or your village. It breathes heavily across every country and every continent.

I certainly know that physical talent exists. It's fairly obvious. Go to any park and watch a group of young soccer players and you will notice that some are better than others. Some will have a better first touch, a greater vision for movement and a more accurate eye for goal. Growing up I myself played with young golfers who found the game easier than I did. They picked up a club and ripped the ball down the middle of the fairway. Their handicaps tumbled down quicker than mine. They drove the ball longer and holed more putts. I found the game phenomenally difficult – I don't think Rory McIlroy does and I don't think he ever has!

The traditional view of talent is a physical one. A soccer player who shows a deft touch, an eye for a goal, or a vision for space is usually declared talented. The 13 year old who scores 50 goals for her team is labelled talented, as is the 16 year old who makes her debut for her National Youth team. However, I'm going to offer you *my* definition of sporting talent. It may not be dictionary perfect but it's my take on natural ability.

Talent in sport is the demonstration of appropriate physical behaviours and appropriate mindsets.

31

Talent doesn't *just* comprise of the young soccer player who excels from the get go, seemingly without trying. That is physical talent, which accounts for only one type of aptitude. Talents are packaged differently and there is an *accompaniment* to physical talent that also exists. That is what makes up the rich tapestry of life as we know it – especially in the world of sport.

My view is that talent also includes mindset. Mindset skills comprise of areas such as focus, confidence, discipline, motivation, self awareness, self management, desire and dedication. The list could go on and on! Mindset talent is crucial in determining a player's ability to acquire physical skill over time – in the medium to long term - enabling a footballer to transit easily from one age group to the next, from youth team soccer to adult soccer. Mindset talents also influence physical behaviours in the short term – how consistently they are displayed and whether they function effectively under pressure. All well and good to be very skilful on the training ground, but the player who shudders with fear come match day soon has a sharp fall from grace.

The concept of mindset talent is one the soccer coach must grasp if he is to develop a creative coaching culture.

Physical Versus Mindset Talent

Coaches can easily fall into the trap of being overly excited about the presence of physical talent – irrationally so. They exaggerate the importance of physical talent and under-appreciate the value of mindset talent. They become too fixated on short term ability (how well someone performs right now) as compared to focusing on potential ability (how good someone can become.) Physical talent present in a young soccer player's game is thrilling to watch, but it is not a reliable indicator of how capable someone is in the long term.

Take the case of two 12 year olds I came across at a local club recently. Both are strikers and both possess the dream of becoming a professional in the English leagues in the future.

A striker called John is head and shoulders above his peers. He excels in and around the penalty area. He is alert, alive and lively the closer he gets to the opposition goal. He displays a vision and ability to find space that is uncommon in a player so young. He strikes a ball cleanly and his shots are powerful. He scores frequently and is marked as a future professional at a leading club in Europe by the coaches who work with him on a daily basis.

Compare and contrast John to the player he keeps out of the team, a striker called Kevin. Kevin is quick but clumsy. He can outpace a defender but sometimes his first touch is poor. The ball regularly bounces off his foot. In the 18 yard box he isn't what you'd call lethal. He scores infrequently. He is small and he tends to get out-muscled by the defenders. He doesn't really look the part and is marked by coaching staff as someone who will most likely be looking for a new, less advanced club in the near future.

Who is going to 'make it' as a professional? Surely a no-brainer, right? But let's add some complexity into the mix. I had the opportunity to speak to both of these players (I was brought in with a remit to help Kevin improve his sharpness in front of goal but had the opportunity to speak with John at a training session). I discovered an intriguing sub plot to the marked difference in their physical talent.

One of these players has an iron will – a determination that knows no bounds. He wants so much to be a professional when he grows up and he's determined to live the lifestyle and put in the hours that will give him the best chance of reaching his dream. His eyes lit up when I spoke to him about practice and extra training. He has been having extra coaching to improve his touch, his dribbling and passing. His enthusiasm has also led him to start physically working out. He's too young to go to the gym, but he's been doing some body weight exercises and he's started to notice a difference (he told me this with a broad smile on his face).

The other player can be quite lazy. He wants to go professional when he's older and thinks it's a dead cert that he will, but as a result he spends more time playing on his Games Console than at the park honing his skills. He chuckles at the ability of some of the other players. He believes only he has the skill to 'go all the way to the top.' His attitude to play is questionable. He wants to do well but if he hasn't scored in the first half he doesn't really bother in the second – he's only interested in scoring a hat-trick. He's only out to impress.

Interestingly, it is Kevin, the less physically talented player, who is the one with an iron will and a willingness to do what it takes to get to where he wants to go. Who do you think has the most appropriate talent now? Is it Kevin or John? John, the Games Console obsessed young player displays the most appropriate on pitch behaviours at the age of 12 but is he likely to keep developing these behaviours? Isn't Kevin going to overtake John? Isn't 'Physically Challenged but Iron Willed' more useful than 'Physically Gifted but Lazy'? In my experience it is Kevin rather than John who has a better chance of fulfilling his long term goals and aspirations.

I am a fervent believer that intelligence (as a branch of mindset talent) is a profound mediator of success in football. I believe you can take a player who doesn't have a natural propensity to develop motor skills or who doesn't have exceptional physicality, but who is an intelligent and motivated learner, and you will probably find that she will eventually catch up to her more physically gifted peers. Physical talent can decline, where mindset talent so often extends.

My argument is simple. In sport there is physical talent and mindset talent. Both are inborn and both can be developed. A coach who wants to develop a creative coaching culture must recognise that mindset talent is as much a mediator of development and subsequent success as physical talent. He cannot allow himself to be blinkered by the physical. He must expand his definition of talent.

The creative coach is a no limit coach. She works with what she's got and finds ways to produce speedy progress and miracle results

Mindset Talent – Born and Made

I believe many elite sportsmen and women, if they are born to be great, do not enjoy this birthright as a result of a genetic gift, such as hand eye coordination or a natural grace in movement, but as a product of an innate temperament to succeed.

Many champions reach lofty heights because they were effortlessly focused when competing as youngsters. Some were born with a positive demeanour that helped their progression stay on course through thick and thin. Others came to the sporting arena with a discipline forged not through motivational tapes but because determination is *who* they are and *how* they are as a person.

Let's illustrate my argument using Tiger Woods. Tiger had some innate coordination – anyone who can play scratch golf by age 13 is physically gifted. But if one were to narrow down to a 'most important' ingredient in the Tiger Woods recipe - to me - it didn't lie in his hands. This was an important component of the recipe but not the crux. More significant was Tiger's in-born temperament. Tiger displayed a level of maturity, motivation, and focus for a youngster beyond his years. Most 6 year olds want to play with a toy truck or action figures. Most 6 year olds who play golf have a minute attention span and are more likely to retire to the side of the green to play with the sand in the bunker than to carry on hour after hour, putting the ball towards a stationary hole. Tiger did this. He was obsessed, focused, motivated and disciplined. 99% of 6 year olds, no matter how good their parents want them to be at golf, won't be Tiger Woods because they won't have the in-born soft skills that Tiger was blessed with.

Tiger's talent was multidimensional – he had a physical gift and a mental ability. He was also fortunate to have an astute sporting father who coached him from day one. As a golf coach I spent hundreds of hours coaching 5-10 year olds. Of the thousands I taught over a 6 year period very few (if any) had Tiger's level of focus. Tiger was talented – but not just physically. Tiger had mindset talent.

The Mindset Talent of Ronaldinho

The Brazilian footballer Ronaldinho had mindset talent as well.

He was born into a wooden hut in a favela in Porto Alegre in 1980 and had an abundance of physical talent from the outset. This was seen spectacularly as he made an instant impact at the age of 7 playing futsal for his local club Gremio. But his inner desire radiated as well. He had a role model close to home – his brother Roberto Assis, nine years his senior he played for Gremio youth team. He also lived a stone's throw from Gremio's spiritual home, the Estadio Olimpico enabling him to absorb his motivation on a daily basis.

He practiced from dawn until dusk honing his skills on the dirt tracks and filthy pitches that decorated the poverty stricken Favela community. As a teenager, Ronaldinho showed great determination and work-rate, and often stayed behind long after training, when Gremio's youth teams had finished, to work on his own skills, set-pieces and crosses. He grew an obsession for the great Brazilian player Rivelino – a fixation that drove his will to become accomplished with his left foot as much as with his more favoured right foot.

Ronaldinho became one of the best players in the world because of a heady blend of physical and mindset talent. With ball attached to feet and burning desire cut into mind he was able to generate skill levels rarely seen on a soccer pitch. And when that mindset got lost in a sea of success Ronaldinho's world class career exited as quickly as it arrived. He is still playing, but it is only his physical talent that keeps his career from drowning.

Ronaldinho may have reached the pinnacle of the game with a mix of physical and mindset talent, but I firmly believe the coach must place a greater emphasis on the role of mindset talent as a mediator of success in soccer. And permit me to present another compelling rationale behind this argument. One which lies in the nature of football itself.

Are the world's greatest soccer players born with it?
Or are they a product of their dreams and a
relentless love of practice

Soccer is a Game for All

Allow a snapshot of the greatest sprinters of all time to rest on your mind. From the iron willed Harold Abrahams, 1924 Gold medal winner who was immortalised in the film Chariots of Fire, to the grace of Jesse Owens, the man who won against the odds at the Berlin Olympics of 1936. From the defiant Jim Hines in 1968, to the all round four Gold Medal winning superstar Carl Lewis, to the untouchable Usain Bolt.

A mental picture of sprinters serves the mind with a sporting cocktail of raw power, lightness of feet, strength of torso - a combination of relaxation and tension with physical prowess in abundance.

Comparing the sport of sprinting with soccer enables us to get to the heart of why football coaches should be looking at mindset talent as a mediator of achievement within football (as well as why they should be optimistic about developing very good players and perhaps several professionals along the way.) Sports like sprinting are closed skill and to a large degree simplistic. Yes this discipline requires sound running technique but from a genetic perspective it requires a lot of fast twitch muscle fibres and that's about it. Football offers a more complex landscape. A soccer player can ease his way into a team with less physicality if he has great feet and learns to think quickly (think Xavi Hernandes and Lionel Messi). Similarly, a soccer player can earn a living from playing his favourite sport if he lacks the ball skills of a Brazilian playmaker but enjoys the gift of height and muscular strength that are synonymous with playing as a centre back. Swift one-twos between his team mates may not be his forte, but consistently winning headers in dangerous positions might be.

The exciting thing about football (and maybe this is why it is the world's most popular sport) is that, when you really think about it, physical factors rarely rule you in, or rule you out, of how far you can go. Of course there will always be kids who struggle to acclimatise to the nature of soccer – I'm not saying everyone is born to play like Falcoa, Iniesta or Hugo Llorente. But the nature and complexity of soccer means that we shouldn't over-value the influence of physical talent on success. How good a player becomes is largely down to their will and their skill – and as a coach you have a strong influence on both.

What Talents are In Front of You?

To be a creative coach you have to broaden your definition of talent. You will have players in your team who can spot a pass and deliver a 40 yard ball flawlessly into the path of a team mate. You will have players whose touch is velvety smooth, players who glide by the opposition, and players who time a tackle like a concert pianist times the notes in a bar. You will also have players who don't possess that kind of skill but who are gifted with intelligence, a passion for the game and a desire to learn and improve. You will have players who dream day and night about dancing with the ball under the lights in the best stadiums in the world – and commit wholeheartedly to developing the brand of game that allows them to eventually do so. These players have mindset talent. They are players you must cherish as much as those with tricky feet. Players with fast feet so often trip up in the mid to long term. Mindset talent can win (and probably will win) over time.

The creative coach understands that talent comes in these two forms – physical and mindset. He has an expansive definition of talent. He then spends himself in a worthy cause – he strives to develop the talents he has in front of him. If he does any labelling he labels what talent each individual has. He doesn't label his player either talented or talentless. To him being talentless doesn't exist. That's a fiction he can't abide. Once he is clear about the different talents different individuals possess he quietly, gently, carefully builds on the abilities his students have.

Chapter 2

As a creative coach I'd like you to take a little time now to think about all of your players. Where do their talents exist? Do an audit of your players as individuals and as team mates. Resist the urge to criticise your players. Simply look deep inside your mind to expose the talent that is displayed explicitly and implicitly in front of you week in week out. You ask for intelligent form from your players, so demand insight from yourself.

This isn't a mind reading exercise. Mindset talents manifest themselves behaviourally. They can be seen and heard. They can be distinguished from their physical counterparts. Here are some examples:

- *The player who remains unflustered after making a mistake*
- *The player who is audible before and during the game*
- *The player who is quiet but offers a physical presence*
- *The player who listens attentively*
- *The player who asks questions*
- *The player who stays behind to do more*
- *The player who simply looks determined*
- *The player who has fun*
- *The player who follows a mistake with determination*
- *The player who watches soccer like a student*
- *The player who can speak of set plays*
- *The player who doesn't stop running*
- *The play who stops running to play intelligently*

All of these (and many more) are behaviours related to mindset talent that can be checked and logged by a coach and used to speed the journey towards excellence. Players who display these behaviours may not execute the game as well as some – but I urge you to be mindful of their importance. They can release excellence in technique over time.

A personal investigation into your players' talents amplifies your creativity because it opens up a new line of coaching enquiry – "How can I magnify the talent this player has so other areas of her game improve?" is one question you might ask yourself. Finding the answer carves the creative coach.

*The coach who understands the talents of his players
can accelerate the learning process*

Mindset Talent Requires Patience

Like physical talent, mindset talents are a product of birth – but these qualities *can* be made. They can be nurtured and developed. Some soccer players are naturally more focused, confident and determined than others. But others have to grow these attributes, just as certain players have to spend more time working to improve their passing, shooting and dribbling skills. This book is dedicated to helping you improve player mindsets. There will be a range of techniques that you can dedicate towards developing mindset talent.

I'd like to get started by introducing you to two coaches who adhered to a formula that set them apart from their coaching peers – a philosophy that not only helped them become creative coaches but also helped them develop both physical and mindset talent.

3
The 1%ers

In 1953 graduates of Yale University were surveyed to determine how many of them had specific, written goals for their future. The answer was a paltry 3%. Twenty years later, researchers polled the surviving members of the Class of 1953 and found some amazing results - the 3% with goals had accumulated more personal financial wealth than the other 97% of the class combined. Incredible!

Incredible but not true. This neat little anecdote that has been told the world over by self-help gurus on stage, and in many of their books, is completely made up. An exhaustive investigation by Yale uncovered no longitudinal research at all. They believe no study took place. They believe it is a myth.

As a sport psychologist I'm not a big advocate of goal setting in its purist sense. By and large people set goals but they don't *do* goal setting. There are very few people who *don't* have targets or goals related to their future, but these tend to be safely lodged in their mind rather than written down in a journal or goal setting book. And of course these goals may change due to personal circumstance. The rigidness of the traditional goal setting process is unrealistic to say the least. Trying to achieve something by a certain date is admirable, but quite often things beyond our control intervene to prevent a specific outcome from happening.

Some people have a concrete set of goals and enjoy having the clarity of purpose this gives them. Others have a vague image of the end in mind but the picture is fuzzy, ambiguous, or open to change.

That's fine. Clarity of outcome isn't always necessary. What *is* important is involving oneself in the process of improvement. As a soccer coach this means improvement for yourself and others. It means a non-stop search for excellence and distinction. Let me tell you a few stories about a couple of iconic coaches who have mastered that search.

Be a 1%er

The kick was struck cleanly - the parabola perfect. And he knew it....

His eyes were wide and his vision fixated on trajectory and as soon as he saw that oval shaped ball puncture the middle of the conversion posts he felt a surge of excitement flow through him.

"World Cup, World Cup," he screamed to one of his team mates. And he didn't even have to collect himself for more play. Time was out and the 2003 Rugby World Cup had been won. Johnny Wilkinson, the England fly half, had sealed it for his country in the last seconds of extra time.

The drop goal he had executed was one of thousands he had put to bed over the previous few years. It had been rehearsed countless times, physically and mentally. For Wilkinson the placement of kicks was routine. They were one of many 1% influences he knew he had on the game. And 'one' was a massive percentage to him. It was a number that had been drilled into his psyche by Clive Woodward, the England rugby coach – the man who had been gently steering his nation towards the top of world rugby for half a dozen years.

The Woodward obsession was minutiae - the fine detail that separates first from second. When he was appointed the National Rugby Coach, England was yet to win a World Cup and the game of rugby was transitioning from an amateur into a professional sport. A recreational approach wouldn't cut it in a brave new rugby world. For England to compete with the powerful Southern Hemisphere sides of New Zealand, Australia and South Africa they had to sweat the small stuff. To become acquainted with victory the nitty-gritty had to be taken apart, examined and enhanced where appropriate. A superior rugby machine had to be built out of new pieces as well as a re-alignment of the old.

With a conveyor belt of new training and match day habits Clive Woodward's team evolved into the number one ranked squad on the planet. Wilkinson's last gasp World Cup winning kick merely cemented their status as the superior power in rugby. When asked to consider the differences between the England team that was defeated at the hands of South Africa in the quarter finals of the 1999 World Cup and the victorious team of 2003, Woodward stated that the heartbeat of improvement lay in doing 100 things 1% better. He didn't suggest that the team grew due to doing just 1 thing 100% better. Assembling success had required a minute shift in dozens of practices and an introduction to small new routines.

So often the soccer coach becomes stuck – a tunnel vision in approach, with thought centred on one way, one style, one system. It's easy for the soccer coach to lack creativity. The 1% approach that Clive Woodward took enforced flexibility in his coaching culture. He squeezed the creative juices out of himself, his coaching staff and his players. He exercised his imagination and unearthed a whole bunch of effective strategies which helped his England team do things better, stronger, faster and with greater confidence.

For you to be a creative coach you must strive to be a 1%er. You must direct your focus and exhaust your mind daily to uncover the things that need to be done better, need to be touched up or altered slightly. This is no fad or craze - a 1%er is successful in all walks of life whether in the boardroom, the theatre, the music studio or the comedy circuit because they differentiate themselves from others. They magnify their strengths and improve on the areas within their coaching culture that require progression. Where there is a successful sports team, and where there is a constant stream of players stepping up to compete for the first team you will find 1%ers at the helm. They are original, they are so often unique, and they are the most creative. They produce champions.

small shifts in anything – mindset, technique, game plan – make a big difference to performance

The Best of Britain

In fact they can produce champions from nothing.

The desolate waste ground of the Great British Cycling team in the late 1990's was a frustration to its new Performance Director, Dave Brailsford. A Gold medal in 1992 and no golds (and just a couple of bronze medals) in 1996 were paltry returns and unacceptable to a championship winning mind. Brailsford had found his life mission – to create *the* dominant force in world cycling.

Brailsford, like Woodward, is a 1%er – a man who is happiest when he's carefully studying a graph or analysing statistics. His brain comes alive when he is in the Velodrome, taking in information, identifying weaknesses, flaws and limitations, then coming to a conclusion and discovering ways to apply what he's learned. Relentless in his approach he slowly constructed one of the greatest winning machines in modern day sport.

The 2008 Beijing games saw the British Cycling Team win 14 medals, 8 of them Gold. After China, the opposition teams said it couldn't happen again. It may not have been a fluke they said, but results were the product of a golden generation never to be repeated, never to be seen again. The British team thought otherwise and they went about implementing a training programme to surprise the world in their home Olympics. Shock and awe was their incentive. In 2012 they again won 8 Gold medals. The country in second place in the medal table only won a single Gold. The British team continue to win medal after medal in World Championships and world records are scalped with an air of ease.

Brailsford's regime was laid down with a simple ethos at its core - the 1%. For the British team the 1%'s were found (and continue to be found) by taking a demanding and honest look at current coaching processes. They extract the 1% *from* everything they do and look for a 1% margin for improvement *in* everything they do. This is a coaching culture that is creative and open minded. If a mechanic fits a tyre on a bike and someone argues it can be done better then Brailsford's inclination is to test this new suggestion, re-test and implement if effective.

The cycling team call this process the 'aggregation of marginal gains' Their passion is simple - the 1% will win by the inch or will win by the one second. When all these 1%'s are added up over time champions are produced. Like England rugby, British cycling's 1%er changed the rules of the game.

The 1% in Action

These rules had been changed for Nicole Cooke as she took her position for the 2008 Olympic Road Race Final. Her modifications were a combination of the subtle - the not so obvious – but they still caused everyone to stare.

Perhaps everyone glanced at her because she looked different. She was encased in a one-piece skinsuit, typically favoured by track riders. The traditional garment in road races had been discarded. She didn't need pockets on the back of her shirt and she believed that the greater aerodynamics properties and comfort could give her a marginal advantage - a 1% difference over the rest of the field.

But maybe everyone stared at her for a different reason. Perhaps it was because of Cooke's choice of equipment. She had decided to ride a bike fitted with ultra-light tyres, of the type, again, favoured by track riders. This was a risk - they are more vulnerable to punctures, especially in the rainy conditions that characterised the women's road race in Beijing. But it was a risk worth taking. Not for her a silver or bronze medal – 1%ers avoid that sport thought. Her second 1% gain was a gamble, but one Cooke felt was worth taking.

As well as looking different Cooke thought differently. 1%ers do! Another marginal gain took place in the heat of battle as the race was coming to a conclusion. The final corner required a sharp turn before moving into a straight and up a hill towards the finish line. Approaching this corner Cooke communicated by radio with the team car; her coaches were worried that, in the wet, using the ultra-light tyres, there was a risk of crashing – a crash that would have brought a cruel end to her challenge for top Olympic honours. So, after liaising with her coaches, she decided to take the corner slowly, smoothly and with care. In the process she lost several lengths to her breakaway companions. But this was all part of her final 1% - she calculated that she could make up the difference. And she did just that, winning a memorable sprint to become the first British road cyclist to win Olympic gold.

This was a victory for the 1%ers and the aggregation of marginal gains. It wasn't the skinsuit alone that won the gold medal that day in Beijing. Nor was it the use of the thinner tyres. Cooke's tactics on the final bend were street smarts that propelled her into the back straight but she had to be in that position in the first place. But taken together, when these 3 1% processes were added up alongside her training and racing programme, alongside the support from her team-mates, as well as her attention to many other small details, it all combined to generate an advantage of significance - a winning advantage.

Chapter 3

The 1% Nudge

I'm unsure that such winning advantages are delivered through 'people change'. I'm not sure I believe in such a thing. I don't think people change as such, and I don't think you can change people. Not from a personality perspective anyway.

I believe that people nudge and shift throughout their life, sometimes towards where they want to go and other times away from the goals they set themselves. I believe the role of the soccer coach is to help a player to nudge and shift in the direction of improvement and toward consistent high performance. To my mind a 1%er is a 'nudger' and a 'shifter'. A word here, a sentence there nudges and shifts. A new drill, a different type of play nudges and shifts. A new pair of boots, a technologically advanced training aid nudges and shifts.

I want every coach to find 1% nudges for their individual players and for their team. I want them to obsess over the 1% nudge. I want their passion to be the 1% nudge. 1% nudges make it easy for your players to improve. They make it easier for your players to score, to defend, to create chances and to snuff out the space the opposition striker might have in the penalty area.

Can you find a couple of 1% nudges for all of your individual players in the next fortnight?

Can you find 5 1% nudges for your team in the next month?

I don't want you to think that my reluctance to believe that people can change is one of pessimism. My thesis is far from negative. Let me be clear, 1% nudges, when added up, lead to big changes in performance. You don't have to change people to change performance, you simply have to provide small nudges to improve players and help teams deliver high performance.

I think that is actually enormously optimistic. I think that sounds simple. I think that sounds like you, the coach, can have a big impact on a player by offering a clearly defined 1% nudge.

A nudge here, a nudge there – produces champions out of also rans

Finding the 1% Nudges

To develop a creative coaching culture you need plenty of 1% nudges. To be a better coach you need a whole pile of 1% nudges. Take time to develop 1% nudges for all of your individual players – they all count. You will find plenty in this book, but you need a whole bunch more - referencing technique, tactical play and game intelligence.

1% Nudges for individuals are so often overlooked in football because training is mostly team oriented. But 1%ers understand that a team is only as effective as the sum of its parts. Ultimately your goal should be to help individual players be the very best they can be. Finding their 1% nudges is a part of that journey. The chapter on building an 'Individual Performance Plan' in the 'Culture of Commitment' section will guide you through that process. It's straightforward and simple and will help you become a better, more creative coach.

Driving Your Culture of Creativity

A relentless dedication to increasing knowledge

Improvement requires knowledge. Creativity requires knowledge. Modern day soccer requires lifelong learning. Be the John Wooden of your generation – make everyday a learning experience.

Be a no limit coach – qualifications are only your entry point into the profession

The greatest coaches on the planet complete their fundamental qualifications then demand to know more. They don't stop learning the day after they pass their licences. They'll never stop learning. Make this you!

Break the game down into its constituent components and build knowledge in each area

Every part of soccer is coachable – every player can improve the different components of their game. Studying the minutiae of performance and building a library of resources in each area helps you become the superior coach.

Look outside soccer for vital clues in the development of coaching excellence

Never inhibit your improvement by isolating soccer from other sports and from other performance domains such as business and science. Search high and low for resources to help improve your players.

Expand your definition of talent – there is such a thing as 'mindset talent'

Talent isn't just physical. It's not just what you see on the outside. What's inside a player's mind is just as important. The nature and complexity of soccer means that you shouldn't over-value the influence of physical talent on success.

Know the talents in front of you

Mindset talents can be seen behaviourally. Look for clues and develop where appropriate. Players who display these behaviours may not execute the game as well as others – but be mindful of their importance.

Be a 1%er

Players improve over time through small 1% nudges and shifts. For you to be a creative coach you must strive to be a 1%er. You must direct your focus and exhaust your mind daily to uncover the things that need to be done better.

Section Two
A Culture of Confidence

You, the coach, are integral to the confidence of your players and your team. Through your actions, your attitude and your voice you shape your players' feelings of confidence – on the training pitch, at home (away from the pressures of training) and under the lights on match day.

As a coach you must help your players feel confident – strong, dominant, committed, decisive, bold and brave.

Confidence can be elusive in the competitive world of sport and soccer is no stranger to its inconsistent shades. One day it can be your teams' weapon – disciplined shape, quick passing between players and attacking flair in abundance. The next match and confidence is a blunt instrument in your sporting war - a sticky midfield, movement lost and sharpness dulled.

As a coach you must bring consistency to your players' confidence – an ever present mental quality that delivers reliability, uniformity, harmony and regularity.

Confidence is the most vital mental component. Focus requires it and intensity feeds from it. It's explicitly seen through motion – a bounce in the step, an upright posture, a freedom of movement, feet with speed, eyes that scan and anticipation that wins and maintains possession.

An ignorance of the dynamics of confidence is not good enough. To be the complete coach you must know how to nourish and nurture the confidence of your players as individuals and as a unit – as a team.

As a coach you must build your players' self-belief. This is the forerunner to confidence – this develops the student of the game, the patient and persistent player, as well as the player who loves to learn the subtle nuances that creates game intelligence.

This next section to Soccer Brain introduces you to a blueprint that holds the keys to implementing a culture of confidence. The formula for a culture of confidence is in 7 simple steps:

1. Believe in the power of self-belief
2. Understand a player's explanatory system
3. Drive philosophies of optimism
4. Build self-belief (don't let them break it!)
5. Have your self-belief tool kit to hand... daily!
6. Know that competence can be wrapped in confidence
7. Expose players to the feeling of confidence and mindset in training

4

The Belief They Need

The 80,000 fans were singing once again. The intense atmosphere was back at the Westfalenstadion and from "The Yellow Wall" came a barrage of noise, passion and excitement. Ticker tapes littered the pitch in appreciation for a Championship winning team – not just a 'one time' team but a back-to-back Championship winning side. The season ending 2012 had seen 24 straight games without a loss, 80 goals scored, and a Bundesliga record for a points total of 81.

Many argue that money is the crucial determinant of success in modern football. But money wasn't the key to this club's resurgence. In fact it was having no money that was its solution and salvation.

Germany's Borussia Dortmund Football Club was a team with power at the end of the 1990's and impressive results in European competitions. But success was built on financial quicksand and by 2008 Dortmund had to sell their stadium, were without star players, and were a mid-table outfit. Enter the little fancied and little known Jurgen Klopp...

The Optimist Coach

Perhaps every great coach has an idiosyncrasy - Joachim Low's cover shoot style, Jose Mourinho's alluring self-confidence, and Arsene Wenger's professor-like form are a few that come to mind. Borussia Dortmund's Jurgen Klopp is famous for, and much loved because of, his sideline celebrations. But whilst the fist pumping is popular amongst fans it is also incredibly frequent – his team is very successful.

Klopp has taken a Dortmund side, with very few resources, from mid-table mediocrity to champions of Germany in 2011 and 2012. They now rival Bayern Munich as Germany's premier soccer team.

His beginnings at Dortmund saw him bring in fresh faces and a pledge to fans that his new team would play with leidenschaft (passion), and Vollgasveranstaltungen (industry and heart). Players soon learnt to compete with speed, to pass without fear, to pressure opponents swiftly and transition quickly.

But for all his technical know how it is Klopp's commitment to the mental side of football that has set him apart from other highly astute coaches in Germany. He fills players with belief through individual care, an exhaustive approach to motivation and inspiration, as well as an insatiable thirst to help players deal with challenges in a positive manner. Klopp loves to help his charges re-frame the negative – a technique I will talk about later and one that, when used correctly, helps the soccer player to see the toughest situations in a positive light.

His view on winning is fascinating – perhaps in stark contrast to some of his contemporaries, but in parallel with some of the latest findings on the psychology of excellence. He wants to win – of that there is no doubt - and he works as hard as any manager to make sure his team have the best opportunity to make that happen. But he has amazed German journalists by telling them that winning isn't everything - that winning a game played poorly isn't always better than losing a game played well, because this kind of victory brings with it a false sense of success. For Klopp football matches aren't one dimensional – they aren't just about results. To him a principle of team and individual development is of greater consequence in the mid to long term. Klopp insists that sometimes defeat is balanced by necessary growth.

With his emphasis on mindset, Klopp has created a team full of confidence. Whether by intuition or intellectual design he has the understanding that a team packed with individuals who believe in themselves and who are capable of playing with a freedom to express, lends toward soccer players who will compete with speed, with precision, with strength, with intelligence and with will. Efficiency and execution - the German way. The Klopp way.

The Klopp in You

It's a very simple shift in coaching mindset. Put the mental side of soccer on a pedestal and you will liberate greater potential in your players, sometimes releasing an ability that can be hidden from view. If scarcity of talent is a complaint from your club's hierarchy, then develop the talent you have – utilise a toolbox of techniques that raises the bar for the average and the also ran. Your players may not become soccer legends but you'll give them a great chance to be the very best they can be. And within your soup of average there most likely lies a golden nugget waiting for you to uncover them.

Fans talk of Klopp as a motivator but in the strictest sense this is only a part truth. On closer inspection he's a teacher of optimism, a coach of building belief. He knows he can't turn bronze into gold but he commits to shining his bronze and his silver so they look every bit as stunning as the gold he cannot afford. The noisy world of technical maintenance and tactical execution hasn't blunted his capacity to surge the power of positive mentality across his squad.

Can you surge the power of positive mentality across your squad? Can you become a teacher of optimism as well as a teacher of technique and game play? Can you help your players reach a point where they are oozing with self-belief? Can your words and your sentences deliver impact – with surges of self belief piercing your players' psychology and physiology?

There is nothing magical about Klopp's approach. He merely believes in the power of the mind. And look at the results he gets. If you want to attain similar outcomes then commit to the same standards of mindset delivery that he does. Believe in belief and believe in optimism. It's a worthy path to take – especially as there are global examples of the irrational and illogical impact that an abundance of self-belief can have on sporting performance.

A great coach liberates; a great coach creates certainty - with a mantra of 'freedom and focus'

The Kenyan Can-Do

Sport anthropologist Rasmus Ankerson has studied some of the best known communities of sport achievers. He has spent time in Russia examining the tennis sensations that have hit the women's circuit over the past decade, and has learnt from the phenomenally successful South Korean women golfers. He has also scrutinized the cultures of Jamaican sprinters and Brazilian footballers.

But it is his stories of Kenyan long distance runners that are the most intriguing. In his outstanding book *The Goldmine Effect*, Rasmus explains that virtually *all* beginner runners in Kenya want to set a world record or win a city marathon – a proposition they believe to be realistic from the outset. The Kenyan running culture is awash with an inherent and unshakeable belief – they will win World Championships, they will win Olympic medals, and they are incapable of losing to a foreigner. Rasmus tells the story of former 5000 metres world champion Benjamin Limo. Limo had no TV, only a radio, but through it he listened to accounts of how Kenyans had won gold medal after gold medal at the 1988 Olympics. This injected what could be perceived to be an irrational sense of confidence into Limo – just by turning up to the Olympics he would win Gold for his country. Of course in reality not all Kenyans returned home with a medal in the Seoul Olympics that year. His primary sources from the radio were somewhat unreliable, but his impression was one of endless victories – a 'self-brainwashing' effect that fuelled his conviction that success in global long distance running was the easy path.

Of course the easy path it never has been, nor ever will be, but when you add the Kenyan work ethic mantra of 'Work Hard, Win Easy' to a mindless optimism and self-belief bordering on irrational you are presented with a lethal combination dedicated to accomplishment. The Goldmine Effect exposes an interesting phenomenon – an equation for breakthrough performances that coaches should strive to adhere to. Hard work plus self belief delivers performance success, while intelligent application plus mindset steers a quicker development path. And the Kenyan 'Can Do' mentality has not only scaled the athletic world, it has also asked questions of the value of sport science.

Data Rich Threat: Going Beyond Heart Rate

If you visit Iten, the home of Kenyan running, you won't see cutting edge laboratories with state of the art sport science equipment. For that matter visit Russia and you won't find the most incredible tennis courts and tennis centres.

Take a trip to Jamaica and you won't see the advanced scientific tools that the UK and the USA use at their National Training Centres.

The Kenyan long distance runners don't have their maximum oxygen uptake measured or their muscle fibres checked. They are not limited or burdened by such information. They simply run hard, with good technique and run with self-belief and victory in mind. It's that simple.

I am a great advocate of the involvement of science within the elite sports environment. I have great friends with great minds doing great things in sport science at sports clubs across the world. But I have concerns. My worry is the limitations of rationality. My concern is that the human dimension of self-belief is lost amid a sea of scientific data. I have stood on the sidelines of a Premier League training pitch and have been told by a physiotherapist and sport scientist that a young player we were watching had little chance of 'making it' because he didn't have the aerobic capacity to play in the first team. Really? If we all competed to the boundaries of what our physiological signatures deem possible then records would fail to fall and human improvement would grind to a halt.

My experience with football coaches treads a similar path. All too frequently player assessment and subsequent potential is delivered too quickly and without all the evidence compiled. "She's too slow", "He's not tall enough", "Her first touch is too sloppy", "He doesn't know how to play his position" are a few of the judgements I hear that condemn young players to the scrapheap.

- *If she's too slow help her play in a position that suits her pace.*
- *If he's not tall enough help him use his height to his advantage.*
- *If her first touch is poor then help her to improve it.*
- *If he doesn't know his position well enough then teach him it – set him homework to learn it better than anyone else.*

It's a simple matter of shifting your coaching mindset from one of 'judgement' to one of 'development'. "What can I do to help" should be your driving creed. No footballer is immune to the process of improvement – everyone kicking a ball can get better at it.

This doesn't mean I believe we can all achieve anything. Such a claim belongs in the library of role-playing fantasy. But I refuse to accept the labelling limitations that some of the science of today (and some of the coaches of today) places on sports competitors. We must all exercise open mindedness onto the impact that willpower, motivation and self belief has on an individual's potential.

Making decisions from data is a dangerous game. Take the person as a whole – avoid overlooking her personal qualities (remember mindset talent?). Examine grit, hardiness and will. Consider the toughness a soccer player has in order to overcome adversity. And reflect on self belief. If these qualities aren't quite up to scratch they can be improved and these in turn will improve physiological capacities. It's not just a one way street – mindset improves physiology as much as physiology mediates mindset. Let me show you how.

The will, the toughness and the grit they show on the pitch is so often a product of how much they believe in themselves

Explanation: The Hidden Moderator

I'm unsure if Jurgen Klopp has ever been to the University of Pennsylvania in the United States but I'm pretty certain he would quickly make friends with one of its most decorated staff members. Professor Martin Seligman is one of the world's leading psychologists, famed for his ability to underpin self-help with scientific rationale. Seligman has, in recent years, helped psychology move beyond a focus on disease and problem orientation towards a field that explores human strengths. His 'Positive Psychology' is a field of study that examines healthy states such as happiness, well being, strength of character and optimism.

At the heart of Seligman's thesis is something he calls 'Explanatory Style'. He points toward 'explanation' as a strong mediator of how optimistic someone is. To my mind, at Dortmund, Jurgen Klopp has developed a coaching culture that helps his players explain the different situations they encounter as professional footballers in a productive, helpful, and positive manner.

What are your players saying to themselves on a daily basis? What words are they using after a training session? Are they optimistic or are they only remembering the bad moments – the chances they missed, the passes that strayed, the tackles mistimed, and the catches dropped?

What are your players thinking leading into a game? Are they immersed in pictures related to pace, power and persistence? Or is their inner voice awash with a different catalogue of images, a prediction of triple X soccer – a movie of their worst imagination.

Seligman argues that we have two explanatory styles - optimism and pessimism. He suggests that these styles mediate a variety of mental states. How we explain a given situation influences how confident we are in that situation and how much self-belief we feel. It induces a happy disposition or a sad disposition. It delivers feelings of helplessness or hopefulness. All of these emotions are important mediators of how a soccer player trains and plays. They also influence how quickly skill is developed and honed.

So let's be clear, how your players explain every given situation to themselves makes a difference to the outcomes you see on the pitch. It makes a difference not only to their mind mechanics but also to their tactical execution. A player with a pessimistic explanation of any given situation will lessen her chance of playing confident football – reduced vision, slower to anticipate, speed of thought injured, decision making damaged. That isn't science, to me that's plain old common sense – but how many coaches are taking this common sense explanation to the training ground?

Scratching the Surface

Allow me to challenge you. I reckon a lot of you are only scratching the surface of your ability to improve your players because you are focused too much on the external – you are only examining what you see on the outside. As a coach you are conditioned to critique what you *see* on the training ground and on match day. But what you *see* is underpinned and governed by the internal – a player's thoughts, feelings and focus.

For example, seeing poor movement doesn't mean that the player is incapable of attaining the kind of movement that top level professionals have. Poor movement might derive from a lack of awareness which might be as a result of a loss of confidence. Reduced confidence might be down to the player being a little nervous or a little intimidated by the opposition. Or perhaps the player wants to do so well to impress you that he has tightened up and started ball watching. There are a host of reasons as to why a player may have poor movement, and physical talent and technical ability are just a couple of them. We will examine the mental conditioning of a player during training in this section but for now I want you to focus on the internal voice away from the practice area.

A player's inner voice doesn't suddenly stop when he leaves the pitch. Perception continues and explanation persists. The player talks to himself on the way home from training. He reminds himself of what happened – as an individual, as a team mate and as a pupil. He thinks about what you the coaches had to say to him – was it fair or was it unjust? Did it inspire him or did it lessen his confidence?

Your words travel with your players everywhere they go. When they are chilling out they will remember what you said to them. When they are eating with their family they will recall your demeanour that day, and when they are driving away from the training ground they will picture your body language and the way you held yourself.

There is a constant never-ending evaluation and explanation of training, of match day performance and of your coaching. A craft of coaching is to help a player evaluate and explain these areas in the most appropriate manner – one that helps them perform and learn. Optimism versus pessimism may be the most important competition you have to strive to guide, steer and direct in your role as a coach.

Everyone has an image of themselves in their mind - we tend to think and act in accordance with this image. Can you improve their image?

Pessimism versus Optimism

A footballer who spends time talking to herself negatively about her given situation will slow down her speed of learning and lessen her chances of playing well on match day.

Do you think a soccer player who is spending time everyday rehearsing negatives and talking to herself in a pessimistic way is going to feel great on Saturday? Do you think she is going to feel strong, fit, dominant, confident, focused and ready?

By all means train your players hard. Put on the best quality sessions you possibly can. But be very clear in your mind about this – your players won't be as ready as they should be for match day if they have a pessimistic explanatory style.

Let's take a few minutes to think about the soccer specific situations when players may perceive things a little negatively, a touch unhelpfully and with some pessimism.

- *Being dropped – "It's really unfair, I don't deserve to be dropped. I may never get back in the team now."*
- *Having a poor training session – "I was awful today. If I keep training like this my career won't progress. What a nightmare."*
- *After a poor game – "I was rubbish, poor movement, no goal scoring chances, no goals."*
- *Over-concern about a game coming up – "I don't fancy our chances against this team. They're so quick, so strong, so tough."*
- *A predominant focus on the strengths of the opposition "The striker is lightening quick, I'll never have the pace or athleticism to stay tight to him."*
- *Worry about the future, such as a place in the team – "I have a bad one on Saturday and I'm gonna lose my place in the team. It's inevitable."*

Some of these inner explanations and conversations may appear at first glance unimportant, even futile. But they are damaging to the self-belief of a player today, tomorrow, next week, and in the mid to long term.

As a coach you have to fix this. This is a responsibility within your role. That is what world class coaches do – they help their players change the story, shift perception, and alter the narrative.

A Coaching Climate Conducive to Optimism

The good news is that the entire contents of this book will aim to help you manage the explanatory styles of your players. There really are a vast number of ways to help your players perceive things in a more helpful manner and a more positive light. That's exciting isn't it? Liberating? In fact, we have explored some already - players lean towards optimism in the creative culture strategies outlined in section one; implementing the techniques and philosophies that will be introduced in coming sections will also enhance their optimistic explanatory style.

In order to grow optimistic mindsets and attitudes in your soccer club it is useful to build a clear set of philosophies that help guide your players' explanatory style.

I want to introduce you to six philosophies – six soccer relevant messages you can communicate to your players from day one. They are root and branch ideas that set the climate of your culture (they are not just there for when a player gets lost in the fog of pessimism). I strongly believe that if you immerse yourself and your players in these philosophies you will help build a team, club or soccer organisation that is engaged and absorbed in optimism.

Improve your mindset... improve your feet

One: Show you Believe

They can see it in your eyes. They can hear it in your voice. They can detect it from your body language. If you don't believe in a player they know.

If you want the fastest, easiest route to managing the self-belief of your players, then allow me to tell you a secret. If you believe in them, they will believe in themselves. Believe in them with all your heart. Allow time for mindless optimism. It's okay to believe the unthinkable for them – they'll love you if you do.

Display a 'can do' attitude. Tell them they can. Use your words and your sentences to illustrate their capability. Draw an imaginary picture of what they can achieve. Make it big and bold and bright for them. Make it exciting.

Sometimes this is tough to do. When you've told a player to do something time and again and they're just not getting it - your patience is tested. Perhaps it makes you think she can't. Well she can – she just needs a few more attempts at doing it or needs to be told in a different way. Make her self-belief your responsibility because she'll never acquire the skill she needs without a foundation of belief. The more she fails the more you should believe in her. Never ever doubt her. Push her to keep going. Push her through her comfort zone.

Showing you believe helps shape the voice inside your players. It helps them speak to themselves in a positive, optimistic manner:

"Coach really believes in me. I love it when he tells me how well I'm doing and that I can achieve my goals."

Strive for this inner voice – you can tell if it's there, and if it is, you got 'em hooked.

Two: An Emphasis on Fun

Slumps are so often a result of a drop in self-belief. The perfect tonic – the antidote for an extended run of poor form is to have fun and enjoy playing football.

As a coach, insisting on fun might seem dangerous – you want your players focused and competing at the correct intensity. But a player can be focused and can enjoy himself at the same time – in fact, to my mind having fun leads to a focused mindset. In contrast I'm unsure that a player can be focused when little enjoyment is felt in the process of playing. Fun is a forerunner to focus. Fun is the undercoat to a glittering exterior. Fun drives the inner voice of optimism. If I'm having fun I feel good. If I feel good I believe I can progress and achieve.

We do, however, have to define fun. Fun doesn't mean 'to mess about'. This isn't what I'm asserting. A soccer player should derive fun from the feeling of competing hard and from learning, as well as from moving, passing, challenging, swerving, faking, shooting and saving. Fun stems from a mindset that is enjoying the process of execution.

A player who has lost self-belief may need an injection of fun into their game. Insist upon this mindset quality. Insist on your players competing on their toes. Emphasise the enjoyment to be had from playing free flowing football. This shouldn't detract from competition, this should harden the battle.

Helping players dance to the sound of fun can silence the inner critic that stifles their play.

Three: A Space for Negatives, a Time to Feel Down

Insist on the positive all the time? No thanks. Not useful and probably not possible. I always tell my players that an insistence on positives at *all times* is counterproductive. It just isn't realistic and, in my opinion, it's slightly unbalanced to expect players to forever think in a positive manner. You probably can't do it and I definitely can't. They most likely can't either. It is not the way we as humans are wired, nor is it the way we have evolved as a species.

We live in a world of self-help – books and podcasts that make us feel bad when we're not high fiving everyone as we walk down the street. We are surrounded by messages such as 'There is no such thing as failure, there is only feedback.' No, there are plenty of examples of failure, some of which are fatal.

Interestingly a social psychologist called Joseph Forgas contends that negativity can help thinking and growth. He suggests that "Whereas positive mood seems to promote creativity, flexibility, cooperation and reliance on mental shortcuts, negative moods trigger more attentive, careful thinking, and paying greater attention to the external world." I agree. Negative emotion is a part of the mixed tapestry of life that delivers success and excellence.

For example, players who want to develop their game need to spend a bit of time in the negative. They need an exact look at what isn't good enough in their game and what needs to go better. They need to watch footage of themselves play and observe weaknesses and take note of areas that need to improve (we will explore a little more of this later.) Your communication must be precise:

"Analysing the weaknesses in your games may seem a little negative at times, maybe even frustrating, and I understand that you may feel a little deflated. But it actually offers an exciting opportunity to understand what you need to improve. And when we start working on those things you'll get a real buzz from the improvement you'll see and experience in your game. We gotta have that bit of pain first...but that's only temporary."

Players also need to be allowed space and time to be a little down after a poor performance. To my mind being a little negative following a defeat or a poor training session is a sign of desire to do well – to compete and to win. Spending a part of the evening reflecting and perhaps feeling a little low is fine provided that players wake the next morning intent on focusing on the positives and analysing what needs to go better next time. A touch of negative emotion in the evening helps bring in a morning of optimism.

Champions build from their weaknesses. They are excited about knowing what they need to do better

Allow your culture of confidence to flourish by tolerating negativity at times. Tell them it's okay to feel down. But ask your players to allocate time in the negative to evaluate their situation.

"We lost and you didn't have one of your best games. You're going to feel a little down tonight and that's okay. Just make sure you get a pen and paper and note down what you feel you could have done better. I have some ideas but I want you to have a think, yourself, first of all."

Helping players to develop optimism requires a toolbox that helps deliver on flexibility of thinking. Players must, to some extent, be able move up and down the positive-negative scale in accordance to what is appropriate at the time. The next chapter is packed full of ideas to assist you in helping them do this.

Four: Hard Work, Quality Work

"Everyone has a different type of brain and everyone has different talents. Not everyone can be Lionel Messi, Ronaldinho, Pele or Maradona. But everyone can be the best version of themselves. Everyone can improve at soccer and we, as a coaching unit, are determined to help you become the very best you can be. That might be a professional or it might be as a very good College player or County player. Who knows how good you can be – we certainly don't know your limits, but we're going to have fun stretching them. If you want to get as good as you can be, you're going to have to work hard at your soccer, and you're going to have to work with focus, with intensity and by thinking in the right way."

A very simple message that gets footballers focused not on whether they 'have it or not' but on working hard and working in the right way – these are the mediators of success not a mysterious innate ability or God-given talent. Yes this exists but so often as a destroyer of dreams rather than a creator of success.

Optimism is a quality switched on by convincing people that they can - that nobody really knows their true potential, and that any potential can only really be discovered when they work hard and they embark on working with excellence. If a player comes to you in a negative frame of mind because of poor play then the solution of fun, hard work and quality work should be close to your lips.

An outlook such as this fosters the spirit of optimism. It helps players face forward, towards their destination rather than away from their goals. Insist on hard work. Insist on quality work. They are the rod and staff of your coaching culture.

"With hard work and quality work anything can be overcome. You can, and you will, achieve to the very best of your ability with the kind of work I will demand from you."

Five: Focus on Strengths

Tell them what they're good at. They need to know.

Nobody is immune from a drop in self-belief. And everyone is partially blinded by their weaknesses. In fact weaknesses can be all consuming. "I'm no good at passing", "I'm no good at tackling" is all too easy to think at times, especially in the mind of the young soccer player.

As a coach you need to remind soccer players of their strengths. You need to immerse them in a world that values their assets. Set aside some time to reinforce strengths with your players. This can be done before or after training. It can be done in person, on the phone, by text message or via e mail. There are so many mediums to communicate with players these days.

Have a 'Strengths Club'. Create an alliance that gives your soccer players a platform to air strengths. A little chance to show off is allowed. Bonding over each other's strengths is fun, belief building and team forming.

Knowing strengths is a form of performance literacy. Players cannot become great without this awareness and knowledge of self. Without it they won't know what to turn to after a poor training session or game. Without it they can drown in a sea of uncertainty. Provide a coaching climate that allows them to wallow in what they're good at.

Six: Fuel from Adversity

In soccer, as in life, bad things happen. Losses are inevitable and poor performances come to pass. This doesn't mean we pack up and pursue another sport. Yet many of your players will feel the urge to do just that, even after a small or meaningless defeat.

This isn't necessarily because they lack mental toughness. It is because they are explaining the situation to themselves in a manner that makes them want to quit. It is a part of being human. You are a coach not just of soccer but of people. Accept their fragilities and move to help rather than hinder.

Failure is one of the strongest mediators of explanatory style. The pessimist sees failure as permanent. She sees failure as her fault. She sees failure as a sign that she is incapable. She sees failure as an indication that she simply 'hasn't got what it takes.'

A coach of mindset provides a player with a different logic. He guides toward optimism by helping a player embrace mistake and to learn from failure.

"Everyone makes a mistake. If you're not, then you're perhaps not trying hard enough."

"Everyone fails. If you don't experience failure then you are not playing with enough freedom."

Just as the best salespeople love to hear the word 'no' on their sales calls from time to time (it helps them get closer to a yes) then I want you to communicate with your players that you want them to experience the pain and anguish of failure.

Make failure a performance fuel in your coaching culture of confidence. It has to be, otherwise you'll never build the kind of belief your players need to have. Fun should follow failure. Focus should follow failure. Devotion to improvement should follow failure. A re-charge of batteries should follow failure.

A player who makes a mistake should shift her physiology – on your toes, lively, alert, sharp, alive.

A team that loses should shift to focusing on the next challenge. Next week will be our week. Next week we will play with fun, freedom and focus. Next week we'll win.

Great players hate failing but they do appreciate failure. With the correct mindset failure forces focus

Your words travel with them

Pessimism paralyzes the soccer player while optimism releases the spark. The coach who commits herself to managing the inner voices of her players is one who can ignite this spark. She can put that glint back in the eye of the player through her words, through her voice and through her actions.

Your players won't always brim with self-belief. And they can't always be optimistic. But the coach of self-belief is always striving to find that flicker amongst the embers. Having the philosophies outlined above will give your players a better opportunity to stride purposefully onto the pitch with certainty.

The optimistic soccer player is tall of height, loud of voice and drives his team mates to compete when last breath has long exhaled. The optimistic footballer suspends the thought of draw or defeat to fight hard until the bitter end. To stand and appreciate this type of mindset gracing your pitch you need to implement the philosophies we have discussed in this chapter. And to complement them you need a toolbox of techniques to build and manage self-belief. The next chapter will give you just that.

5

Your Self-Belief Tool Kit

Place yourself by the side of a pitch. Not just any old pitch – choose the pitch at the Estadio Santiago Bernabeu where Real Madrid play their home games. Look towards the game – it's Madrid versus Barcelona. Make sure your internal camera is directed out through your eyes – make this image first person. You are alone, standing in the technical area. Now glance around you.

There are 85,000 fans encased in the arena. They are chanting, singing, waving flags – urging their team on. Make this image big and bold and bright. Indulge your senses - allow them to absorb the imagined experience. Make it noisy – deafeningly loud. Immerse yourself in this moment.

Now start to coach the match in front of you. Notice the speed of the game – the intricate passes, the movement off the ball, the runs in behind the defence. Allow yourself to join in - coach from the sidelines. Let the emotion of the game flow through you, but still keep your wits and your sensibility about you – you have to make decisions. You are the manager of Madrid. You are coaching one of the world's biggest clubs. Stand tall, powerful and dominant. You are in charge; you are the master of ceremonies.

Now shift your mind to the last minute of the game. It's one all. Watch as your team starts to move up the gears as they launch one final assault on the opposition's penalty area. A ball played out to the winger who, as bold and as brave and as skilful as can be, takes on the full back. He rounds him and whips the ball in. The crowd can see what is coming and you can see what is coming. Watch from the side as your striker launches off the ground, hangs in the air above his marker and heads the ball as powerfully as his neck muscles allow. Watch as the keeper helplessly dives with arms outstretched, narrowly missing the ball as it shoots past him, with net bulging before he hits the ground.

Now listen. Hear the roar reverberate around the stadium. Join in. Bellow your joy with all the might your lungs will allow. Clenched fists, knees bent, body arched – celebrate to the music of the fans.

How does that scene make you feel? What sensations did you experience as you went through the process of imagining that intense, emotional world of top level football?

As a coach you are the guide of the intellectual *and* the emotional. You must ingrain tactical nous and technical ability, but you must also help players summon up the feelings of high performance. You are part teacher and part cheerleader in a world that is part science, part art and part theatre.

You have to help them think, and you have to help them feel.

It's not all Cogito Ergo Sum

When pondering the nature of existence, the 17th century philosopher Descartes said "I think, therefore I am" ("Cogito Ergo Sum" for all you Latin scholars out there). Descartes argued that the brain was a reasoning machine with no link to emotion. For him, feeling was not part of the process of logic. Descartes never played soccer!

Football is played in the heart as well as the mind. When I use the word heart I'm not just talking about having the will to win in that last lung busting 10 minutes. And I'm not just talking about having the want to track back for the 50th time in a match. I'm talking about the *feeling* of performance.

Great soccer requires a cocktail of positive feelings that emanate from the body. A heady mix of dominance, competitiveness, influence, control, and certainty will go a long way to securing a high performance.

As it so happens Descartes was embroiled in a battle of minds against a philosopher called Spinoza. Spinoza believed and argued that mind and body were inextricably linked and that feeling played a crucial role in intellectual processes. He insisted that reason was shot through with emotion.

Science today is demonstrating that Spinoza had a more accurate assessment of experiencing the world. We have a 'feeling brain'. We think as we perform but we also *feel* as we perform. And how a soccer player feels influences her game intelligence. Without a feeling of commitment it becomes harder to execute the key responsibilities she has within her role on the pitch. Without a feeling of certainty it's more difficult for her to play with her brain – to see, to anticipate, and to make quick, effective decisions. Mind and body fuse to release high performance.

The Feeling of Knowing

In my opinion self-belief is the *feeling* of knowing. It may pull on thought or reason or logic, but it's primarily an intangible source of emotion that fuels performance.

- *I know I can deliver great crosses*
- *I know I can move and lose these defenders*
- *I know I can split open this defence with my passing*

When I work with a player who lacks self-belief I know I have to help this player *feel* differently about her game. I know her inner voice and her inner pictures have to adjust to change how she feels about her game and how she feels about herself in relation to soccer. I know that she has to start knowing that she can. In short she has to cut off the pessimistic explanations of the world around her and the negativity that is embracing her football. This is an important process because there is a strong relationship between a player's everyday self-belief and the performance confidence she feels and demonstrates on match day.

Let me pose this question. Do you think that if a player rehearses failure Monday through Friday that she is going to perform to a high level come match day on Saturday? Do you think the goalkeeper who sees himself drop every single catch, who reckons on a poor game at the weekend, who only remembers his mistakes, is going to stand tall on Saturday? Is he going to dominate the area with his voice and his physical presence? Is he going to command his backline and be drawn from his line decisively when a striker runs in behind his defence?

The soccer player requires an exact feeling of self-belief going into a match if she is to guarantee a performance with confidence. And for this to happen she needs to rehearse success. She needs to explain away the negative or embrace the challenges that come with tough times. She needs to create a mental blueprint of the triumphs of her past and spend time rehearsing the plays that will give her a future full of accomplished performances.

Too many of your players dwell on what has gone wrong in training. Too many of them exercise a mindset of failure leading up to a big match. Too many internalise disappointments and use them as evidence that 'they can't' and 'they won't' and 'they will never be able to'. Too many of them who have the skill consistently fail to show the will. This isn't down to a lack of motivation, but more because their appraisal system lets them down. Their appraisal barometer is fixed firmly in the negative. And too many of your players fail to build skill at the pace you'd like them to – not because they lack physical coordination or an aptitude for the game – but because they are burdened by past failure and future insecurities.

The highest form of confidence is to KNOW. I am confident I will play well, I believe I will play well, I KNOW I will play well.

Building or Breaking

Are your players building or breaking their self-belief?

"Did you build your self-belief today?"

This is a mantra I repeat time and again to my clients. I want them to construct a way of thinking that assembles a strong sense of belief. I want their thoughts to evoke images that help them feel like they can. Too many of your players will chip and chisel away at their self-belief. They probably spend their days breaking self-belief rather than building it.

In contrast some get stuck in neutral mode. They neither break nor build. They train, they play, but they don't use their mindset to reinforce their self-belief. They are not proactive with their self-talk or their internal pictures. They don't stretch themselves mentally and take time out to exercise their brain.

I urge you not to become fixated on the idea that psychology is purely about dealing with problems. This is far from the truth. Psychology is also about helping normal functioning people surpass the expectations of others (and sometimes their own expectations). It's about taking a journey away from the comfort zone and away from the ordinary.

I propose to you that, as a coach of soccer, you should be helping players utilise their mind to build a vibrant and robust self-belief. I believe that you can never help them build enough self-belief. Players can always 'top up' how they feel about themselves and their game.

Remember the concept of mindset talent? Mindset can be built. Its walls can be reinforced. It can be nurtured, managed and cultivated. And you, as coach, are the mental surgeon on the front line. You can help players direct their mindset towards excellence. They need a mental structure – and this is how you can do it.

Your Tool Kit

The 21st century coach has a tool kit to support players in the process of building and maintaining self-belief. The structure and functioning of the brains of your players require you to use these tools – in fact you should be opening your kit almost daily.

The grey stuff tends to attract the negative. Ask a soccer player post training about his worst moments and his best moments from the session. I can take an educated guess that the player will coherently and succinctly whittle off a whole bunch of mistakes while really having to think hard about his better moments. The brain loves to send us in the direction of error. It bookmarks failure and highlights the disappointments. Letdowns from team mates are also red marked.

Your trade as coach is made more difficult by the subtle nuances of the brain. It's prowess to distract can get in your way. It prevents your players from feeling the kind of belief they need to learn, improve, develop and high perform.

The 20th century coach avoided the soft skills that developed the hard skills. He ignored the thinking below the action. He ignored the feeling underneath the behaviours. Be the 21st century coach who cares. Be the coach who knows that the brain of a player wants to stick like superglue to the bad stuff, and be the coach who has the remedies to detach the errors from the brain.

I'm going to give you four tools for your kit. Learn them, understand them and apply them individually, and with your group.

Tool One: Perception - Scaling

One of your players has had a couple of bad games and reports a loss of self belief. He is feeling pretty low, down on his luck. A useful process to take him through is called scaling.

Ask the player this: "On a scale of 0-10 with zero being no self-belief and 10 being full of self-belief, where are you now?" Given that the player has reported a loss of belief it's likely he'll say a pretty low number. Perhaps he might report back 4 out of 10.

Now is your chance to re-frame his mindset. Instead of feedback such as "Well 4 is pretty low" I suggest you respond by being positive and enthused at such a high number: "4? Really? That's great. Why as high as 4? What have you done to get it this high? What's been going well enough to edge your mark up to 4 instead of 1 or 2?" This counter enables the player to look at his situation in a different way. He can now explore the things that are going well. You can start a conversation that highlights the good moments from the past few days.

Him: "I'm at 4 because I did some nice things in training today – made some good runs and delivered some quality crosses."

You: "Fantastic. Tell me more about the runs and crosses. What did you do to spot and time your runs? What did you do to make those great crosses?"

This is a great conversation. You are immersing him in his best moments. You are asking the questions that help him blow these moments up in his mind. Help him get descriptive:

You: "When you whipped the ball into the box how did that feel? What sensations did you get off your boot?

Him: "A great feeling. I love to cross it in with some whip – it makes it really tough for the keeper to deal with. Off the boot it felt like a great strike always does – a feeling of nothing."

You: "It sounds strange but can you get that feeling now, in your mind? Can you feel a great strike off your boot and see a whipped in cross?"

Him: "Yeah, it's weird but I can. It feels great"

Now it's time to accentuate the positives from this exchange so far:

You: "You know I've noticed how good your crossing has been of late. The fact I've seen that also suggests you've been getting more crosses into the box – that's so important. We really want you to get loads of balls into the danger zone and you've been doing that. You should remind yourself of that – you're doing exactly what we want you to do."

Him: "You know I hadn't realised that. I actually feel a bit better just knowing that. Thanks."

Complimenting is a much underestimated tool in coaching. In fact many coaches are scared of being too complimentary. They feel it will give players a 'big head'. They feel it will create laziness – if I compliment him, he'll believe his own hype. Some coaches think that it serves more purpose to criticise than to compliment. They feel this is a more productive form of feedback.

Coaching correction should always be present in any given training session. But correction without compliments will tip your footballers towards the negative. You need the right amount of both, at the right times.

Job done! But not quite! Let's go in for the kill. Let's help this winger focus forward. Let's help him start to focus on the things that will help him keep moving towards improved self-belief:

You: "It's great you're feeling a little better. It's now time to start focusing on the future rather than dwelling on bad things from the past. I have a question for you: What does 5 out of 10 confidence look and feel like?"

Him: "Well I feel that now - after what you've said"

You: "Ok great. Then let's think about 6 out of 10. What couple of things can you do to get to 6 out of 10?"

With this form of discourse you are helping this player become a solver of problems. You are helping him focus on the things that will help him shift and nudge his self belief-up even more. You are placing the onus on him to find solutions.

Him: "I remember we spoke about keeping great body language. I know in the last game that slipped my mind. I need to keep on top of that. I also think I need to be braver taking players on."

You: "I agree about the body language. That is something I can help you be aware of in the next few training sessions. We'll also do some one v ones either during or after team training next week. We'll make sure that you're taking players on. Remember to use your body weight when you take players on – when you shift your weight you pass players with ease."

Him: "I'll remember, thanks."

You can't sprinkle magic dust on a player's head but this exchange comes as close to an instant change of perception and subsequent shift of feeling that you're looking to help players with.

A few confident pictures each day slowly add up to a catalogue of pictures over time. Imagining a confident performance is time well spent

Tool Two: Perception – Compliment the Specifics to Highlight the Strengths

In percentage terms how much do you compliment your players?

Have a long hard think about this question. I bet it's low, very low.

This is natural. Coaching is so much about correction and the climate of soccer coaching tends to be towards the critical and away from the complimentary.

But have a think about this for a few more seconds. You want your players to learn, and learn quickly. And you want your players to compete at their best come match day. For this to happen you need a squad of players to be full to the brim with self-belief and self-belief doesn't materialise in an overly critical environment.

I'm unsure why the soccer coaching environment lends towards excessive criticism. Perhaps it's because we live in a society that shies away from complimenting others. It's a competitive world so why tell others that they're good at something? Alternatively it might be because of the negative brain. It's easier and less effortful for a coach to communicate what is wrong rather than what is right or what is good. Just as the brain is brilliant at remembering our own errors, it's talented at pointing out other people's errors too. It takes some effort to think about and convey what others have done well and what others are strong at.

Quite simply you should be striving to compliment every single one of your players at least a couple of times in every training session. You don't need to take them aside (although doing this a few times a month would be great). Conveying compliments from the sidelines is enough.

Important inputs to player perceptions should not revolve around general complimentary messages. "Well done" may be construed as a compliment but, whilst useful, it isn't that powerful in changing perception, and not necessarily effective in building self-belief. A broad 'well done' isn't specific enough to really shift emotion.

Compliment the specifics. Scaffold down as much as you can:

"I love the way you got up and down the pitch in the last game. You really worked hard and it showed great awareness to be in the right place at the right time"

"Your movement in and around the box was really lively in the training session yesterday. You made it hard for the defence. Keep that up."

"You kept great body language on Saturday when we went a goal down. I saw you – head high, vocal with others. We need that and I think the team reacted well to how you held yourself."

To pierce the skin of emotion and shift self-belief you have to get down and dirty in the specifics of what you see. Be precise, be detailed. Ambiguity only leads to the player perceiving you to be disingenuous.

Tool Three: Memory – Moments to Remember

Why do we have a memory? What is its point? Quite simply memory is the brain's sketchpad for future behaviour. Memory lays down our personal rules for the future – make sure I do this, make sure I don't do that.

In soccer our brain loves us to bookmark and subsequently remember failure. When we have a poor performance the brain attaches a lot of emotion to the experience - it's saying to us "avoid playing like that again because it's gonna give you a whole lotta pain if you do." And so the brain lays down the tracks of this poor performance and jolts our mind every now and then to remember the poor game. The trouble here, as you may have noticed, is that in the process of laying down these same tracks time and again, the brain is damaging our self-belief. It's saying 'you can't' and 'you won't'. It's immersing the mind in a world of disappointment.

What is worth remembering?

- *A player scoring a goal or a striker bobbing and weaving her way through a tight defence – these are moments to remember.*
- *A goalkeeper stretching with a finger tip touch on the ball to steer it clear of goal or a goalkeeper rising high above the heads of the opposition – these are moments to remember.*
- *A defender with a last ditch tackle to prevent the striker from getting in on goal and the defender who gets in front of his man to head clear from danger – these are moments to remember.*
- *A midfielder, head up, spotting the killer ball and playing it with precision; and the midfielder, on her toes, finding space to receive the ball, lending it, then getting it back again – these are moments to remember.*

Moments to remember are those moments that you can use to evoke a strong positive emotional reaction from a player. Like a bolt of electricity flowing through the body, a minty fresh moment of excellence can supercharge the brain to restore self-belief.

I suggest you offer a 'moment to remember' time in every training session. It might be a minute or two before a session, during practice or after training. Gather your players together and share in the experience. Ask them to remember their best moments from the past week (or from the past hour). Ask them to make their images big and bold and bright. Ask one or two of them to share. Make it succinct, make it brief and quick. Throw in some compliments to reinforce their internal perspectives. Help them bask in the glow of thoughts about their best. Shield their moments to remember by offering some of your own. Make this a moment for the individual and a moment for the team.

Just one picture of their best performance in their mind gives them a small injection of confidence. Mindset medicine!

Tool Four: Imagination – Key Words Drill

Excellence in any walk of life is powered by surges of imagination.

Imagination steers self-belief by asking what could be. It tests reality and asks questions of where we are right now. Coaches use imagination in their training by default. Introducing a new tactical shape requires a soccer player to envision what she hasn't pictured before. It demands the player piece together experiences from the past and bend them into a new pattern and structure.

I'd like you to become an expert of imagination. It's a vital ingredient when educating the footballer's mindset. Squeeze all you can from their imaginary pictures:

- *What do the most incredible, sharp saves look like? How do they feel? Picture 10 out of 10 reaction times for your saves. Now turn up the volume. Picture 12 out of 10. Now 15 out of 10. What does that look like? How does that make you feel?*
- *As a striker what are you doing to score 10 goals in a game? What kind of movement do you have? How are you finding space? What does the power in your shots feel like? What does incredible movement look and feel like? Tell me about body shape, body weight and direction.*
- *As a defender what does rock solid look like? What are you doing in the air? What are you doing in your challenges? Stretch your imagination – what does it look and feel like when you are first to the ball every time, when you win every 50/50 and when you keep every striker in your pocket.*

Your players will never perform like the 'full blown maxed out bend their mindset' images that you are trying to get them to imagine. But this isn't the point. You want to help them feel great. You want to trick their minds. You want them to release messages into their brain and nervous system of the impossible – because self-belief thrives on unimaginable excellence. Because they will feel unbeatable when they tread the turf on match day. Because they will release a cocktail of chemicals that shoots positive emotion through the logic of the responsibilities within their role....

....and because they are better served thinking about a game tinged with the unlikely than dwelling on the chances of playing poorly in their next competitive encounter.

A key ingredient to helping players use their imagination lies in the questions you ask them. Use the words 'what' and 'how'. And help them have a richer sensory experience by using words such as 'look' and 'feel'.

Have your players be specific about detail. It's tempting to brush over the surface and accept vague descriptions – but if your players' inner pictures are laced with ambiguity you are not impacting their mindset and being as influential as you can be.

Power confidence through them by getting them to exercise their imagination on a daily basis

Back on the Pitch

Tapping memory and imagination and directing perceptions are your stalwarts in managing your soccer players' self-belief. They combine to create the sum of a player's thoughts. Become skilled at leveraging these components of thought and you will become an expert at managing the feelings your players experience in and around training, on match day and after the game is won or lost.

The self-belief toolbox is especially for those coaches who think that a player has self-belief or doesn't. As you have read, you *do* have ways to adjust its volume and to switch it on and off. It's not a mystical quality. It can be massaged through words and it can be influenced through sentences. It is the effectiveness of the interaction you have with your players that makes or breaks the belief they feel.

Interaction is so much of coaching. The balance of success and failure often comes down to the gap in-between player and coach. The right communication in this space is a fundamental every coach should practice time and again. This holds true for match day relations as well as for off pitch contact. But it's the training ground messages that are so vital. Let's head out there and see if we can change a few mindsets.

6

Training with Confidence in Mind

He may have been 42 at the time but he tried his best to keep up with them.

The sprints were from one end of the pitch to the other – and back again. Lung busting gassers designed to sort the men from the boys. Of course he didn't have to join in, he was the boss. But his philosophy was simple – never ask the players to do something you're not willing to do yourself.

Sprinting behind the pack mattered little to Coach Don Shula at the time. His participation in training was a ploy to communicate one of the many messages he wanted the team to understand, and when he had first arrived at the then hapless Miami Dolphins his players needed them.

They also needed to sweat the small stuff. Along with Shula's willingness to get stuck in during training he was a details coach to boot. He possessed a fine eye for the minutiae and regularly stopped training to ensure players weren't succumbing to small mistakes. In Shula's world there was no such thing as a minor error – these simply led to disastrous outcomes.

Don Shula's energy and fixation on small details were richly rewarded. Within two years of his arrival he led the 1972 Miami team to the 'winningest' season in NFL history with a 17-0-0 record. His positive approach and his positive attitude combined with a crossing of the t's and a dotting of the i's enabled him to instil a game winning confidence that helped his East Coast team set a record that is yet to be equalled – and perhaps never will.

As a details coach, Shula was a student of coaching confidence. He knew this mindset wasn't turned on easily in his teams. He was right, confidence is unpredictable. Its volume is erratic and a nudge or a shift either way can lay claim to having dramatic consequences for performance. There is a fine distinction between a player who demonstrates it in abundance and a player who has lost its magic. Every coach is aware of its potent powers but many pay lip service to developing it. Involvement in the process of establishing performance confidence is not enough. Its onset requires commitment from player and coach – a combined personal investment to building and maintaining its walls. Involvement simply won't cut it.

A Plate of Bacon and Eggs

A plate of bacon and eggs is a plate of commitment and involvement. Whilst the hen is involved… the pig is committed! Coach Don Shula didn't take the straightforward road – he was always committed, just like the pig. This road requires a slightly more complicated map, a few more twists and turns - but it's the road I want for you in your education as a coach of mindset. It's all too easy for a coach to be the hen, to take the effortless path - set up the practice drills, lay down the rules and let the players get on with things.

I want coaches to be pig-like, to be committed in the training sessions they serve. I like them to be greedy. This doesn't mean barking out from the sidelines in an aggressive manner nor does it mean an over-abundance of words and sentences. Guided learning may be a coach's preferred style, with less instruction the norm, but even an approach that places the student at the centre of the learning process demands an emphasis on intelligent feedback - the coach's voice is still a necessary steer in the teacher-pupil relationship.

The most important components of your soccer education are the hows, the whys, and the dos of technique, formation, pattern and shape. I believe that and have no problem admitting it. The great coaches are great tacticians. They introduce solid organisation across the team. Their training sessions cultivate the art of attack and defensive structure. They examine every detail of tactical performance.

But the systems designed, developed, integrated and executed by the mind and voice of the great coaches must be wrapped in the teaching of mindset – the coach must parcel her players' competence in a thick layer of confidence. Let's be clear, competence by itself is not enough to produce the elite player, nor the winning team.

The Confidence Wrap

A coat of confidence covers the layers of player skill and game intelligence, pressure proofing and readying them for match day. A spread of confidence also builds these most important game components - skill and intelligence in soccer fail to develop effectively without the confidence to change or to take risks. It can feel uncomfortable to change technique so a degree of confidence to do so is necessary.

A coach who wants his players to shine under pressure and perform with confidence must do so by establishing a clear set of mindset strategies that are implemented before the game so they can be applied during the game.

Do you as a coach know a number of simple tools and techniques to prepare your players to compete with confidence?

It's not enough to simply say to your players "let's play with confidence." Yet many coaches the world over only have these four words to fall back on.

So far in this first section you have new philosophies and techniques that aid your coaching culture of confidence. You have a variety of tools to develop the self-belief of your players – for it is self-belief that initially drives performance confidence. The footballer who has belief in her ability to meet the demands the game throws at her is a footballer who is well placed to go into a game with a high level of performance confidence.

Now we are going to multiply the opportunity you will give your players to compete with the utmost confidence. This is an art and not an exact science – your players will have difficult days, times when the ground feels tacky and when the ball doesn't want to do what they tell it to do. That is the life of a soccer player and we *all* have to accept that. But there are simple ways to help your players experience and build performance confidence. You can help your players practice the *feeling of confidence*.

You want to increase a player's confidence? Insist on great body language and loud communication. The outside drives the inside!

The Feeling of Confidence

The champion golfer stands on the first tee and stares down the middle of the fairway. She feels strong, dominant and decisive. She feels a wave of confidence flow through her body. She looks around and sees her opponents. She inwardly smiles – looking at them makes her feel even more confident.

The champion tennis player walks onto the tennis court and feels a burst of energy. He sees powerful shots and un-returnable serves. When he treads onto the court, whether it's clay or grass or a hard surface he senses excellence. He senses athleticism and strength. He feels confident.

No matter what your sport, confidence is a feeling. It's a sensation. It's built partly through intelligent application in training, partly through self-belief training, and partly through preparedness and readiness to perform. When I work with a soccer player I know that half the battle won is to equip him with a set of strategies that raise his confidence thermometer. This is the job of a coach too.

To my mind a key component in helping players develop the confidence to perform is to *understand* that confidence is a feeling. Although it's partly driven through intelligent application, confidence is the physiological signature of positive emotion surging through the body.

Let me repeat that because it's important to grasp the concept. Confidence is the physiological signature of positive emotion surging through the body. It is a positive physical response to a given situation.

That feeling of confidence can be experienced anywhere in the body. It's very individual specific. Some feel it in their chest – a warm, oozy glow that covers the heart and rib cage area. Others feel it in the feet – the feeling of speed, agility and quickness. Some goalkeepers feel a spring in their step. I've even experienced a defender tell me that he felt confidence from his back – his back felt strong and secure, like a piece of iron. He explained that this feeling drove his defensive duties – no one was getting past him or in front of him.

This may seem like an abstract concept, but I urge you to think back to your playing days. I'm sure you had matches when you walked out onto the pitch and just *knew* you were going to play well. You *knew* that success within your role was a given. And you will have likely felt that in some part of your body or maybe multiple parts of your body.

As a coach I would like you to help players experience these sensations. I'd like you to help them live, breathe and consume these feelings. I'd like you to help them make these feelings habit.

Experiencing Confidence

When competing as a professional golfer I took the last couple of putts on the practice green, before any competition round, from no further than two feet away from the hole. I wanted to see the ball hit the back of the hole and collapse into the darkness. I wanted to hear the ball bounce on the bottom of the cup. This sensory blast would send a wave of confidence through my golfing body – see the ball go in the hole, hear it go in the hole, and feel the stroke that would send it there. Perfect!

This idea wasn't mine, it was a process many golfers would go through just prior to teeing off. Some did it religiously – they wanted to have that experience of the feeling of confidence to send them on their way to the first tee.

It was during my coaching career that I started to give the 'feeling of confidence' any real thought. I stumbled upon it while giving thousands of lessons to ordinary amateur golfers who barely had time to practice their game. I quickly realised how redundant teaching the mechanics of a putting stroke was if my instruction didn't involve some sort of confidence training. Technically, I would set the situation with clarity – stance and posture bent into perfect position, grip naturally laid onto the club, stroke fluid back and through on an ideal path. But to piece the movement together I needed the human controller to *feel* confident – to *feel* able to execute the stroke I had taught her. Without confidence the rhythm, timing and tempo of the technique wouldn't be there. The technical elements would fall apart. An inefficient motion would ensue.

So as a part of the process of my lessons I would teach the feeling of confidence. I would ask my clients to putt (or swing) with confidence.

Show me a confident putting stroke.

Pay attention to what that feels like. Where does that feeling come from? Are there any words that sum up your feeling of confidence as you stroke the ball into the hole?

Let's re-create that a few times.

This 'feeling of confidence' process helped my clients experience the execution of their new technique wrapped in a layer of confidence. I wanted them to immerse themselves in this feeling. I knew that the more they felt this, the easier it would be for them, not only to execute their technique with confidence (under pressure), but also to climb into a feeling of confidence on competition day.

I firmly believe that experiencing confidence is a crucial but little thought of process in sport coaching. I'd like you to introduce it into your training sessions. You must become the master controller of confidence.

Where coaches can go wrong is to separate the tactical, technical, physical & mental sides. They are inextricably linked

Insist on Confidence

Whenever I'm delivering a workshop and I get to the stage when I'm talking about training confidence I usually make a quip saying that if the audience was to take *just one thing* away with them - then this message would be the one I would deem most important:

When you train your players, insist on confidence.

So how do you, the soccer coach, do this? You do it by using the words *confident* and *confidence* time and again as the drills you set down are played out before you.

In fact, I'd go so far as to suggest you demand that your players execute *everything* with confidence. The ideal is for your players to *deliberately* execute everything with confidence. As your players train, ensure you attach the words *confident* and *confidence* to the technical and tactical elements of the game.

- *"Show me confidence – I want to see confident passes – drill it into your mate's feet."*
- *"Show me confident body language – head up, on your toes, let's see lively. On your toes, on your toes."*
- *"Show me confident vocals – be energised and energise others."*
- *"Show me a confident first touch – ball out of your feet, then clip it into your mate. Move towards her confidently – show me confident movement."*
- *"Let's be confident in the air guys – like you've won that ball already. Come on I want to see a confident leap, a confident head on the ball. Get your head right through it, attack it!"*
- *"In this keep-ball exercise I want to see confidence. Head up, that means confidence. Vocal, that means confidence. Making runs and having lots of movement. Showing for the ball, that means confidence."*

Why is the insistence of confidence one of the most important messages you can send your team members? Because we ask players to play with confidence yet we don't set up situations when they can experience confidence? If you fail to help them get used to the feeling of confidence they can't re-create it when it most counts. It's a little like someone asking you to build an unassembled wardrobe without an instruction manual.

The 21st century coach includes the words confident and confidence in her coaching time and time again. He loves his players to experience touching, controlling and playing the ball with confidence. He surges a volley of positive emotion straight through the bodies of his players as they drill, as they practice and as they train.

"I want to see confident body language. Yes that's it – confident actions. Show me. Let's see confident movement. Show me. Every touch must be confident. Every pass must be confident. Show your team mates how confident you are. Show me how confident you are. Feel as confident as you can be."

This communication tool is relevant in every single training session. It's both prevention and cure. As much as a slump in form is a habit of 'no confidence', so a coach can create a habit of confidence. It's simple! It just requires an insistence of action with confidence, body language demonstrating confidence and movement displaying confidence. There are no PhD's stuck to this concept and yet coaches consistently allow slumps in form to rise to the surface of a player's game. An emphasis on fun, an insistence on freedom of all actions, and a resolution of confidence during training is the perfect antidote to slumps and a wonderful tonic that helps develop consistency throughout a player's game.

Confidence on the ball is a result of playing with freedom and being decisive. Help them think & train like this & they will play like it

Insist on Mindset

I have deliberately emphasised the insistence of confidence during training. This is a section about developing a culture of confidence at your club or within your coaching structures. But don't let me mislead you. It is possible and very practical for your players to enjoy instruction enveloped by every aspect of mindset.

"I want to see a focused first touch. Focus on the ball and on moving it just out of your feet. Then make sure you're clipping a confident pass. Then move to the next cone with intensity – be vocal along the way"

This sentence alone introduces the player to several important mindset messages – be vocal, focus, play with confidence and maintain intensity.

Repetition of these words is crucial for players to be able to build into their training vocabulary. They need to become instantly recognisable and they should be on the lips of players as they train and as they compete. But your insistence helps things go beyond the intellectual and into the emotional. It helps players *feel* what it's like to focus, to play with confidence and to compete with intensity. That is what you want them to experience because that is what you want ingrained in their psyche and in their heart and in their feet.

- *"Show me some intensity on this exercise. Work, work, work. Head up, receive the ball, release it then make space to get it again. Feel that intensity. I want this intensity repeated on match day. Work with intensity, work with intensity. This is what I want on the pitch."*

- *"Focus when this corner is taken. Pick up your man and focus on him and the ball. Remember it's a split focus from man to ball, ball to man. Success as a defender here is all about focus. Focus on the right things and you'll give yourself a great chance to win the ball if it comes near you. Focus on the right things and it will give you a great chance to stay a step ahead of the man you are marking. Remember, it's all about focus."*
- *"This drill is all about reading play and thinking ahead. Remember, the best players are able to read the game – they are 2 steps ahead of everyone else. Reading the game requires playing with your head up and anticipating what you see. Focus and confidence are crucial here. Focus and confidence. Always alert, always sharp, always focusing on the play ahead, and always thinking "what next?" Focus and confidence are what we are training here."*

This is a different set of instructions to what may be considered the norm. Here we are emphasising mindset to bind technique and tactics together and give our students the best chance to execute with the correct mental components.

A coach must help a young footballer develop both competence AND confidence. It is skill AND will that drive consistent high performance

A Chicken and Egg Scenario

I often hear the lamenting of a coach whose team is on a losing streak. "If only we can get a win – that will fuel our confidence." Do you recognise the problem with this philosophy? To win you have to play with confidence, yet the manager is relying on a win to unburden his players and enjoy the benefits of confidence built from the victory. Well which one comes first? If this is the prevailing belief then nobody would ever win because nobody would ever have the confidence to win.

It's a chicken and egg scenario.

To win you have *to be* confident. It's not a case of *we have to win* to be confident – that's illogical and if you want to be the complete coach then that can't be your style. This attitude, this belief, must be an unacceptable philosophy in your coaching process.

Instead of seeking this type of mentality seek to introduce new words into your coaching regime. Unlock a catalogue of inner pictures that can drive the mentality and mindset of your players. Your players don't need to win to develop confidence. They don't need to win to improve focus. They don't need to win to deliver future performances full of intensity. They don't need to win to be the best they can be the following week. They don't need to win to learn effectively.

What they need is your voice. What they need is a constant injection of energising words that supercharge their actions. What they need is a soccer world full of pick-me-ups that release incredible body language. What they need is fun and freedom and focus. They need sharp and alive and alert. They need quick and urgent and intense. They need want and will and desire. They need bold and brave and drive.

They need your voice guiding their outer and inner world as they train. They need your belief and your attention. That must be there in abundance. That is a culture of confidence.

Driving Your Culture of Confidence

Believe in the power of self-belief

Improve the Klopp in you and build your players' self-belief. This is a much underestimated process and evidence from sporting excellence around the globe suggests that those who believe in themselves can achieve extraordinary things.

Understand a player's explanatory system

Develop a coaching culture that helps your players explain the different situations they encounter as professional footballers in a productive, helpful, and positive manner. Help them become optimists.

Drive philosophies of optimism

Show players that you believe in them, place an emphasis on fun, give them a space for negatives, work them hard – with quality. Show them their strengths every day, and use adversity as a fuel to learn and perform.

Build self-belief (don't let them break it!)

Too many of your players will chip and chisel away at their self-belief. They probably spend their days breaking self-belief rather than building it. Players can't build enough self-belief.

Have your self-belief tool kit to hand... daily!

Coaching self-belief is tough because the brain loves to attach itself to negatives. Your tool kit should be opened every day. It consists of memory, perception and imagination. Create a world full of self-belief.

Know that competence can be wrapped in confidence

You want your players to play with confidence but do you insist on them experiencing the feeling of confidence in training? Every training session is an opportunity for them to feel a surge of confidence flow through their body.

Expose players to the feeling of confidence and mindset in training

As your players train, ensure you attach the words *confident* and *confidence* to the technical and tactical elements of the game. Make your voice be heard. Insist on seeing confident passes, confident challenges, and confident movement.

Section Three
A Culture of Commitment

You, the coach, are integral to the commitment your players and your team demonstrate on and off the pitch. Through your actions, your attitude and your voice you shape your players' feelings of commitment – on the training pitch, at home (away from the pressures of training), and under the lights on match day.

As a coach you must help your players feel committed – strong, dominant, determined, decisive, bold and brave.

It is difficult to show full commitment for 90 minutes. Soccer introduces the player to problems every second of every game – problems that sap energy and reduce hardiness. Sometimes it's a game of chance, sometimes one of skill – soccer is variable in its outcomes. No matter how good your players are - their patience will be tested and their frailties will be exposed.

As a coach you must introduce your players to a mental structure. You must help them understand their mindset and mind-state in the moment, and improve their ability to adjust accordingly. A shift in state is a shift in playing standards!

Commitment off the pitch is tough to maintain. To be human is to be inconsistent. Your assistance is required for players to stay moving forward and to remain straight of path. Coaching the individual within the team is of paramount importance if your team is to function optimally.

As a coach you need to be inspirational and your communication should embrace aspiration. Every player counts. You need to set in motion a plan for your players to be the best individuals they can be and the best team mates they can be.

This next section in Soccer Brain introduces you to a blueprint that holds the keys to implementing a culture of commitment. The formula is simple:

1. Understand the difference between the challenge and threat states
2. Embrace power poses for yourself and for your team of players
3. Use match scripts for all your players
4. Love to train the individual
5. Adopt and execute intentional practice in your training sessions
6. Ask your players to write training scripts
7. Develop their ruthless streak through mental contrasting

7
Developing the Ruthless Competitor

As she passed the 1,000 year old Tower of London her inner voice drove her on. History may have been by her side but it was also in front of her.

"This is just a half-hour run now, I can do this," she whispered to herself.

And so she kicked on. There were swathes of people lining the streets to cheer her every step. They were enjoying the English runner leading her home marathon, but they probably didn't realise they were witnessing one of the greatest performances in athletic history.

As her feet continued to stretch the pace so her inner voice remained constant and steady. She drove back feelings of pain and stomach cramps by directing her focus onto neutral stimuli – she counted to 100 again and again. As numbers drifted in and out of her consciousness she was able to maintain the feel for her pace as the metres, the yards, and the streets flashed by. With an iron will she preserved her unrelenting speed, running the 24th mile in 5.03 minutes and the 25th in 5.08 minutes. She would cover the last 800 metres in a mere 2.25 minutes.

When Paula Radcliffe crossed the line to win the 2003 London marathon, expert commentators could scarcely believe their eyes. As she staggered under the finishing banner, the clock above her head showed 2:15.25 beating the previous world best for the women's marathon by just under 3 minutes. An astonishing feat by a woman whose heart was designed for fitness and whose head was tailored for toughness.

As a sport psychologist I believe the most significant factors in her performance that day were her ability to deal with the pain she felt beyond the 18 mile mark and her capacity to maintain an extraordinary pace, the like of which had never been witnessed before in the women's marathon. This was mental gymnastics exemplified. Despite the soreness vying for her complete attention throughout the race, she kept a body wracked with ache and hurt functioning to its maximum capacity. For the thousands of hours of training to weave their magic it took an inner focus on numbers – a continuous count to one hundred – to displace the pain and to touch athletic history.

Paula Radcliffe, the greatest marathon runner ever was in a certain state of mind to achieve the impossible. She was in a Challenge State.

The Unknown American

The unknown American was in a challenge state as well. It was 1964, it was the Tokyo Olympics, and it was the 10,000 metres.

He was on the final bend of the last lap. In third place behind pre-race favourite Ron Clarke, and Tunisian Muhammad Goumadi, the unknown American was experiencing some weird sensations. His vision was blurred and he felt tingles running up and down both his arms. His self-talk was strong:

"One more try, one more try, one more try."

As he came around the bend and into the home straight his inner voice changed:

"I can win, I can win, I can win."

Still in 3rd place with 40 metres to go he felt a surge of adrenaline pour through him. His body tingled. With every stride he felt stronger, faster and more powerful. His inner voice changed once more:

"I've won, I've won, I've won."

And it was then that the cocktail of hormones he was releasing into his bloodstream took effect. As he drove for home his supercharged body set every muscle into overdrive. His body relaxed, his legs exploding with speed, his mind attuned to the finish line. Billy Mills, the unknown American, scorched past the Tunisian and Ron Clarke to take an extraordinary and very unlikely Gold Medal.

Billy Mills was unknown because he had little pedigree coming into the race. His best time for the 10,000 metres, four years previously at the Tokyo Olympics, was a cavernous two minutes slower than the times that were winning the event in the early 1960's. But he saw things a little differently. His goal became simple and two-fold. Firstly he had to train at a greater intensity – he had to consciously stay on top of his pace a few more times each lap. His second goal was one of mindset – he had to believe. He had to believe the impossible and the unlikely. So he set about seeing his victory in his mind every single day, dozens of times a day. He kept a diary and noted his weekly progression for future reference.

By the time of his Olympic race he was in a challenge state, and he stayed there from first gun to the final lap bell to the finish line. Nothing and no-one was going to move Billy Mills from the challenge state – nothing and no-one.

The Challenge State

Footballers respond in one of two ways to a competitive fixture. When a soccer player perceives and appraises the competitive situation in a positive manner he sees it as a challenge. When he perceives and appraises the match in a negative way he sees it as a threat. In a challenge state motivation is high, focus of attention is good and physical functioning (technique) is efficient.

How many of your players see match day as a challenge?

How many of your players see match day as a threat?

In a challenge state a footballer gives himself a better chance to execute his role and all the responsibilities within his role. So the goalkeeper in a challenge state is more likely to make great saves, get in the right positions while his team is in a defensive situation, catch crosses, command from the back, be on his toes – alert, alive, sharp and ready. The striker is more likely to have the kind of movement that finds great positions to score. The defender is more likely to get to the ball first when it's being crossed into the danger area.

The message is clear – your players will execute the responsibilities within their role effectively and efficiently when they compete in the challenge state - when they perceive and appraise every given situation in a positive light. I spend much of my professional life by the side of the pitch looking for both challenge and threat states. Their differences are both obvious and subtle. Here are some common behaviours, mindset qualities and physical signatures related to the states:

- *Challenge is moving, threat is static*
- *Challenge is vocal, threat is silent*
- *Challenge is working hard (in the right way and at the right time), threat is lazy or headless chicken*
- *Challenge is freedom, threat is fear*
- *Challenge is head up and checking shoulders, threat is tunnel vision*
- *Challenge is quick anticipation, threat is slow to spot space*
- *Challenge is showing for it, threat is hiding*
- *Challenge is overlapping (when appropriate), threat is staying back (when not appropriate)*
- *Challenge is relaxed and composed, threat is uptight and tense*
- *Challenge is alert, threat is flat footed*
- *Challenge is strong in the tackle, threat is weak in the tackle*
- *Challenge is being ready and up for it, threat is making excuses and self-handicapping*
- *Challenge is fast, threat is slow*

These two states should become your best friends. As a 21st century coach you need to recognise their form. Knowledge of the state your players are in, as individuals and as team mates, is a mindset basic.

Be clear - a player doesn't simply lock into a challenge or threat state. He will start in one or the other with his state shift dependent on his perception and appraisal throughout the game. This is constant – just as football is a game of movement so the mind perpetually moves. And how a state shifts over the course of the game is determined by what is happening on the pitch. This, in my opinion, is the birthplace of inconsistency – a player not managing his state as he plays and as he competes. Increase the pressure - say a cup final or a play-off game, and a player's state becomes even more difficult for him to manage. This is where his toughness comes in.

Player perception is so much of the game. How he appraises the situation determines his mindset

Toughness and your Two States

Toughness is in everyone. There isn't a person on this planet that cannot *do* tough. Some find it easier than others. Perhaps they were born this way, with ice in their veins. But everyone can learn tough, no matter what their background, their experiences, their values or beliefs.

Mental toughness isn't a mythological quality that is for the chosen few. That's pop psychology. That notion belongs in the films of Hollywood. Toughness is a learnable skill. It can be manufactured and nourished on the training pitch. It can be reinforced on a daily basis. It can be nurtured and improved on match day.

Let me tell you a little secret about toughness. How a player develops this mindset quality is a simple matter of direction and re-direction. It is about shifting and switching in an instant, in the moment and before the second is up. It's about moving back into the challenge state in a flash and it's about staying in the challenge state when everything around you wants to force you into the negative.

I repeat to my players time and again:

You play in the challenge state. Nothing and no-one takes you away from it – nothing and no-one. You compete only in the challenge state. If you come out of the challenge state into the threat state you shift straight back into the challenge state.

This chapter (and this section) will help you build a culture of commitment by helping your players play tough. The techniques you will learn will help you coach them for the challenge state. It will improve your ability to shift them out of the threat state. This is as difficult to teach as it is easy to say, but it is still possible. They *can* manage their playing mindset. You *can* develop a culture of commitment.

BAM Your State

It's frustrating isn't it? One match your players compete in the challenge state – but the next match can be one long exercise in threat state play.

Football will always be played with fluctuation. That is the way humans work, that is the way the nervous system is designed. But the gap between best and worst performances can be lessened. It is possible to help your player immerse themselves in the challenge state and stay there more often. It is possible to have them on their toes, moving, running, making tackles and being active when it would be so easy for them to fall into the threat state.

I'd like to start your challenge state journey by giving you a simple technique to help them manage their mindset as they play. I call it 'BAM your State'. In fact I'm regularly on the phone advising my clients to get BAMMING. I want them BAMMING from the moment they grace the pitch. I want them BAMMING in the warm up, throughout the first half and into the second half. To BAM is simple – it stands for:

- *Body*
- *Action*
- *Move*

I like my players to keep their *body* language positive at all times. I like them to constantly look for an *action* to execute. And I like them to keep on the *move* as much as possible.

Picture that now – your players maintaining incredible body language as they compete. Their eyes are scanning the pitch and their thoughts are focused on the next action, the next play. To add to this they are on their toes - alert, alive and ready. They are always looking to move and always ready to move.

Does this picture paint the challenge or the threat state to you? How can you help your players do this more often on the pitch? Is it an instruction to give them? Should that be done in training, in the match warm up, or at some point during the game?

How you deliver this is up to you. You may insist on BAM during training. It may be a player must-do in the match script. There are many ways to introduce this concept to your team to develop your culture of commitment. I think you should - there is compelling scientific evidence that underpins the BAM process.

*After a mistake...explode into action, after you go a
goal down....explode into movement. Your body
releases your mindset from doubts*

The Power Pose

I'm unsure if Harvard researcher Amy Cuddy enjoys watching a game of soccer.
What I do know is that she'd be dismayed at some of the body language she
would see out on the pitch if she was to take a little look at a game.

Cuddy is an Associate Professor at Harvard University who is fascinated by
bodies. Not lifeless corpses but fully functioning, moving bodies. Her research
has targeted the effects body language has on hormonal change and the
subsequent performance effects. Her findings are dramatic, illuminating and
should have an impact on all our lives.

In her research Cuddy placed participants in a number of poses she labelled as
'power poses'. To give you an idea of what they looked like one was called 'The
Superman' (picture Superman having just landed near a disaster situation, hands
on hips, standing as tall as possible, chest pushed out - I think you get the
picture!) Essentially she was asking people to fake dominance and to fake power.

Cuddy asked participants to hold these power poses for a couple of minutes and
then she measured any hormonal changes that might have taken place over this
short period. She discovered that by simply placing people into these powerful
positions participants had an increase in testosterone levels and a decrease in the
stress hormone, cortisol. The power poses also increased the participants' appetite
for taking risk. Cuddy demonstrated that our bodies can change how we think and
how we feel. Our bodies can change our mind.

*Your footballers can use their body language to change how they think and how
they feel. They can use body language to change their minds.*

Cuddy furthered her research by showing that a change of body language and
subsequent hormonal shifts can make a difference to performance. She had
suspected that it was in evaluative situations where a difference would be seen
most graphically. So she set about testing her theory and indeed found that those
who went through a process of power poses before a job interview were more

successful during the interview process than those who were asked to portray low status poses before an interview. She claimed that the difference between the two groups (low status and power pose) was that the power pose interviewees showed greater presence. They spoke passionately and confidently and they were more captivating and looked more comfortable.

In short, act powerfully, think powerfully and develop the potential to perform powerfully.

You can help your players act powerfully and therefore think powerfully. You can help them to perform powerfully

It's Inherent in Us

Take a little time to picture an image of Usain Bolt winning the 100 metres Olympic final. 'Watch' him cross the line. What does his body language look like? No doubt you are envisioning arms held aloft, back slightly arched, and head held high. This is a position called 'pride'. It's a stance that Jessica Tracy, an associate professor at the University of British Columbia, has studied in detail. Her research has shown that people who are born with sight and people who are born with congenital blindness (blind from birth) both demonstrate this pride pose when they win at a physical competition. Even those who are blind from birth, and who have never seen anyone raise their arms aloft when crossing the finish line, will celebrate in this fashion.

Body language drives our brain as much as our brain drives our body language. As I say repeatedly to my clients:

"Your physiology changes your psychology as much as your psychology changes your physiology."

It's a powerful two way street of personal effectiveness. And it's a determinant of the ability to manage state in the moment. That is BAM. That is the tool your players need.

*Use the wires between your mind and your body.
Keep that two way conversation flowing in the most
upbeat, positive way possible*

The Soccer Body

"Nothing and no-one takes you away from your challenge state but if it does I want to see BAM. I want to see incredible body language. I want to see you ready for action. I want to see you on your toes and moving.

It is your body that will keep you focused and confident and attuned to the right intensity levels. It is your body that must lead. It is your body that slows to relax and it is your body that accelerates to work harder."

The 21st century coach drives her players' body language. She keeps them upbeat and sharp and ready and alert and alive. She keeps them BAM no matter what.

- *You make a mistake...BAM*
- *You go a goal down...BAM*
- *You go a goal up...BAM*
- *You play against a gigantic centre back...BAM*
- *You give the ball away...BAM*
- *You play the league leaders...BAM*

On your watch, nothing and no-one takes your players away from the challenge state. They stay in that state by keeping incredible body language. They stay BAM. If they do veer into the threat state they shift their body language. They get back to BAM.

This is such a simple concept to relate to your players (and I suggest you do!). But it's not always easy for them to execute. If your team goes a goal behind, many of your players will drop their heads. BAM becomes the last thing to focus on. You have to make it their first thought. If a player makes a couple of mistakes in training her thoughts dwell on the past and her body slumps. She slows up. She becomes all consumed by the mistakes. It's tough for her to get her mind back on the game. It's difficult for her to get back into the present. For her to think about body language or BAM in this moment is enormously challenging. This is where your coaching comes in. Specifically, your communication with her. This is when you can offer practical support. She's not weak or incapable of being tough, she just needs some guidance. She doesn't need to be shouted at – she's doing that herself. She needs a practical idea to help her get her mind and her game back in gear.

"Keep that body up. Keep moving, keep working, and stay alert. Stay up, stay up. Let your body drive how you feel."

Help her shift away from the negative back into the challenge. That is your job, and that is the influence you need. That is coaching.

Of course body language can only get a player so far. They have a game of pressure to be played. They have a match to execute with confidence, focus and at the most appropriate intensity levels. Players need to be able to take their training ground game onto the pitch with them without over-thinking or under-thinking. The coach needs a strategy to help players slip into the challenge state quietly and effectively before they grace the stage.

While body follows mind so mind follows body. Becoming aware of the nuances of your body language is a starting point to maintain it positively

Match Script: Where Confidence, Focus and Intensity Meet

One of the conundrums I regularly come across when speaking with both players and coaches is the question of what a player should think about as he plays. Should he think about all the responsibilities in his role or should he not think at all? Should he just be 'looking and doing' or should there be some tangible thought processes behind the actions he takes?

Another playing problem I'm questioned on lies in the match-training dichotomy. Coaches often ask me to help their players take their training mindset into match day. They see players compete with freedom and train in a fearless manner during practice, but come match day a different player emerges - one less likely to take risks, one who plays with shackles on and one who is burdened by pressure.

Similarly, players come to me and ask about the process of preparing for a match. Does a kick off at 3pm require a morning of quiet, visualisation, and alienation from the world? Should a player immerse himself in the game 6 hours before kick-off or should a player relax and allow his mind to drift onto other areas of his life before that moment of truth?

How does one prepare their mindset for a game? How does one deal with pressure effectively? And what should a player be thinking as he competes? How does he effortlessly climb into the challenge state? And alongside body language (BAM) what can he do to maintain playing in this state (and shift back from the threat state)?

To answer these questions I will begin at the beginning.

Control

When your players look at the fixture they have coming up - what do you think might flash across their mind? What inner pictures do they get?

When your players step off the team bus and take a look at the pitch what are their first thoughts?

When your players start to warm up what are they thinking? What are they focusing on as they play?

These are important questions to ask yourself. As a 21st century coach of mindset and coaching culture, how your players are thinking, as well as where their focus of attention lies, should be of paramount importance. This is because your players can slip into the threat state if they are thinking about the wrong things or are focusing on incorrect stimuli.

A crucial determinant of challenge state play lies in the things we can control, the components of the game we can only influence and the areas we can't control at all.

Players can get stuck in 'can't control' mode. In this mode of play they are overly concerned about the weather, the state of the pitch, the time on the clock or on other factors that they can't fully control. These examples sound obvious and yet how many times do players allow such aspects to dictate their mindset? How many times do they allow them to let the threat state slip into their game?

Players also have a tendency to overly focus on things they can only influence. The outcome, scoring and keeping a clean sheet are factors they can influence but not completely control. Winning tackles, headers and accurate passing are similar – they can only be influenced and are not within a player's total control.

The point is this – players who think too much about, or focus too often on, the components of the game they can't control, or which they can only influence, will have a tendency to move into the threat state.

- *They go a goal down – threat state*
- *They play on a poor pitch - threat state*
- *They play away from home – threat state*

The challenge and threat state apply to you as a coach as well as to your players. When do *you* slide into the threat state? Do you become overly worried about the outcome of a match? Do you dwell on refereeing or linesman decisions? Do mistakes from the first half occupy your mind during the second half? The 'out of control' features of a game and those you can only influence are important determinants of your mood and mindset as well.

Players and coaches need to have a simple set of thoughts and focuses as the game is played out. They both require an attention on the things that they can control. As coach the only thing you can control on the side of the pitch is *you* – being the best individual you can be, and the best coach you can be. *You* are the only thing completely within *your* own control. No one else is – not the referee or the supporters or the opposition or your players. Just you!

And it's the same for your players. All they can control is themselves – as individuals and as team mates. To stay in the challenge state they need to keep their mind firmly locked onto themselves and onto the components of their own game.

As the match plays out you need to focus on being the best you that you can be. Nothing and no-one else should change that. You must maintain the challenge state. You must be the best coach you can be.

Players need to do this as well. And as their coach you can help them. The exciting thing is that there is an abundance of things for them to think about and focus on.

Building skill and managing your mindset should be your only obsession. Winning, results....they are just uncontrollable outcomes

Goal Setting

I don't think there is a first session with a player that goes by without me asking this simple question:

"What are you trying to achieve during a game?"

I get a range of answers depending on player position. Normally they refer to goals such as: winning the game, having a good performance, scoring, keeping a clean sheet, winning headers, and completing all passes made. The problem here is simple – none of these are completely controllable. You can't control winning and you can't control scoring. And in your role as a goalkeeper or defender you can't completely control keeping a clean sheet. You can certainly strive to – but it's not something players in those positions can control. If a goal of a centre back is to keep a clean sheet and a team mate makes a mistake that leads to a goal then it's not necessarily something the defender could have controlled. He may have been powerless to stop this eventuality. And so what happens? He heads straight into the threat state lessening his chances of maintaining his form for the remainder of the game.

This is a simplistic view but so often true. The performances of many players are damaged mid game because of a mistake or series of mistakes either by themselves or by their team mates. Their inner voice changes! It shifts from 'can' to 'can't'. They release a cocktail of chemicals into their bloodstream that suppresses their play.

Are you helping your players set controllable goals on the pitch?

As I've already discussed, whilst I'm not a big advocate of some of the concepts within goal setting theory, I do think it's important for players to have goals during a game. But not many coaches set the type of goals that help players play with the correct mindset. In fact many coaches abuse goal setting theory. They choose to set *winning* as their team goal. They choose to demand a clean sheet from the goal keeper. They choose to insist on 'no mistake' or 100% pass completion. This is the kind of coaching that hinders rather than helps. Goal setting is more complex than that – especially if you want your players to compete in a challenge state.

Outcome, Performance or Mastery

A goal can be related to outcome, performance or mastery. An outcome goal is obvious. An example would be "I want to win". As you now know, an outcome goal is one to be avoided. It can be influenced but not controlled (and let's face it, outcome goals are the most obvious things to set anyway – everyone wants to win!!). A performance goal relates to in-game accomplishments such as scoring, making tackles, making saves, heading, and going on runs. At first glance these seem like great goals to set – "my goal is to score" or "my goal is to win all my tackles". But as discussed these fall into the trap of being out of a player's complete control.

So if not outcome or performance goals, then what? Coaches must help their players set mastery goals. These are goals they can control. These are goals they can get their teeth into. They are goals that can focus their minds and allow them to play and compete in the challenge state. Let me give you a few examples:

- *Be vocal at all times* (I can be vocal at all times – that is something I can do no matter what.)
- *Stay on toes* (I can stay on my toes, even after a mistake. I can control this.)
- *Quick, sharp movement* (I can constantly look to move into a new position. I can keep moving at all times.)
- *Get great body shape* (I can control my body shape even if my team are five goals down.)
- *Strong jumps on headers* (whilst I can only influence whether I win a header, I can control the strength of my jump.)
- *Command my back line* (I can be dominant with my voice even if we've just conceded.)
- *100% intensity throughout* (I can maintain my intensity from first to last minute.)
- *Head up - check shoulders* (I can do this relentlessly. I can completely control this.)
- *Make runs in behind – gamble* (I am able to look to make runs in behind. I can gamble no matter the score, the time or the pitch I am playing on.)

Do you recognise the defining characteristics of these mastery goals? They are all controllable. They are all components of the game that have been scaffold down to critical essentials – essentials that players can control and execute no matter what – no matter the time, the opposition, the pitch, the size of crowd, or the weather.

These are the type of goals you need to help your players set. Sit down with them. Or, if there is no time to set individual meetings, email them and ask them to set their goals. Give them some guidelines – instruct them on what they can and can't control. Guide them through the challenge and threat state. Help them become absorbed in controlling what they can control.

Avoid making their goals ambiguous. "Great decisions" is not a sound goal because it's not specific enough. What decisions do you want them to make and when? How can they make better decisions? What have they done in the past that has helped them make good decisions? Mastery goals must be narrowed down to things that players can *actually* do. They must relate to specific behaviours.

A focus on a particular outcome makes
that outcome more unlikely.

Mastery = Behaviour

Behaviours on the pitch are everything. They are the movements, the gestures, the plays and the attitudes you instruct. Mastery goals are behaviour driven. Let's examine some more:

- *Take players on – be brave*
- *Keep my head up - Stay alert and focused*
- *Take quick shots*
- *Focus on strike on shots – make them powerful*
- *Baffle the defender with movement – non-stop action*
- *Authority on corners – take action quickly*

These are all tangible, controllable behaviours that players can take with them onto the pitch. I suggest you help players create two or three plays in their script. For younger players you can stick with one (and do bear in mind older players may thrive on just the one play).

Measuring behaviour is the primary way to judge performance. This means the script is a process that links mental and physical performance. There is a perfect juxtaposition - players focus on their script which can involve behaviours related to mindset. Mental skills can be expressed in behaviour form. Here are some examples:

- *'Checking shoulders' is related to confidence*
- *'Non-stop movement' is related to intensity*
- *'Keep your head up at all times' is related to emotional management*
- *'On your toes' is related to both confidence and intensity*

Of course there can be more abstract plays in the script such as 'Stay in the present moment' and 'focus on the ball' but even the output of these can be seen in action through behaviour. The player who fails to stay in the present moment will be slower to the ball, less active and will look lethargic or overly intense. You can *see* he is thinking about the wrong things in the moment.

The behavioural plays in the script must have another commonality. They must avoid the negative and they must be expressed positively.

Goal Orientation

None of the scripts my clients write contain the word 'don't'. I *don't* let them write the word 'don't' in their scripts. "Don't concede" is a destructive phrase – it develops pictures of conceding.

When players set goals related to what they don't want to happen they are setting 'avoidant' goals. Avoid avoidant goals at all costs. They are negative and unhelpful. They promote the wrong focus by getting players concentrated on the wrong things. The plays in your players' scripts should be set in an 'approach' manner. What is the difference?

- *Approach goals are front foot football – avoidant goals are back foot football*
- *Approach goals leads to freedom – avoidant goals engender fear*
- *Approach goals help players play to win – avoidant goals help players play not to lose*

Players with avoidant mindsets commit performance suicide. They play back foot football. They play with fear. They play not to lose. Do you recognise these styles of play? I do. I see these styles week in week out when a team goes a goal up or when a team goes a goal down. I see avoidant play when a player makes a catalogue of errors or when a player is making her debut. I see avoidant play when I watch a team play away from home and sometimes when they play *at* home.

I have no doubts you've seen avoidant play. This type of play leads to self-handicapping.

Always focus on the things you have to do to win, rather than the things you have to do not to lose

Self-Handicapping

Self-handicapping is a major complaint of many coaches. It relates to when a player shies away from a given situation. Let me give you a soccer example - a young player who is about to play a team at the top of the league may make some kind of excuse before he plays. He doesn't want to play. He doesn't want to make a mistake and look stupid. He thinks the players he will play against may make him look exactly like that. He may feign an injury. In this way he can always make an excuse at the end of the match – "I was injured so I couldn't play at my best." Or he may put in less effort. Logically he knows this might get them into trouble. Logically he knows this isn't the right thing to do. But emotionally he isn't able to cope with the enormity of the task ahead. So he 'goes avoidant'. He shifts into the threat state. He backs off. His whole game suffers.

One of the solutions to self-handicapping in football is to provide a player with a match script. This can help him ignore the great players he is about to play against in the great team he is facing. It can help him focus on what he *can* control and what he *can* do to have a good game. It can help him focus on himself!

"Ignore the opposition – they are nothing to do with you. Remember what we've discussed – keep great body language and keep on the move. You've practiced that in training and I've seen you do it brilliantly before. If you do that today everything else will fall into place. Focus on your match script."

Does this guarantee a sparkling game for this young player? Absolutely not. Does it mean this player is going to turn into the next Lionel Messi? No, of course not. But it *does* give this player a better chance to focus on the right things during a match. It gives him a better chance of competing in the challenge state. It gives him a better chance of being approach rather than avoidant. Ultimately that is all you can help him do.

Pressure Proofing – Making Things Routine

Another benefit of the match script is that it can help your players and team perform under the pressure of match day. It can become a critical essential in shaping the routine your players execute leading into a game.

I'm often asked by clients for a formula for game day. They want to know what they should think about as the match approaches. My response is always the same.

To start with it is important to avoid thinking about soccer until a couple of hours before kick-off. The reason is simple. The brain and nervous system cannot tell the difference between what is real and what is imagined. When a player thinks about playing and performing on the morning of a game she will start to release adrenaline. Spending time thinking about the match will exhaust a player's adrenaline load. If your players look lethargic in the warm up to a match, or from the kick off, a complete depletion of adrenaline levels prior to the start of the game could be the primary reason. To avoid this it is important to ask your players to remove their mind from the match or from soccer until shortly before the game begins.

The match routine starts two hours before kick-off, and it starts with a review of match scripts. If kick-off is at 3:00pm then 1:00pm is a great time to put their match scripts in front of them. It's a great time for them to get that injection of adrenaline before warm-up. Ask players to build a picture in their mind of playing at their very best. Ask them to envision sticking to their match script no matter what. If you've introduced the concept of the challenge state to them ask them to picture this:

What does this look like? What does this feel like? What are you doing in the challenge state?

Ask them to think about what might push them into the threat state. This isn't a negative question, it's a practical question. The threat state is a reality - it *will* happen. Ask them to imagine themselves shifting from threat state back into the challenge state:

What does this look like? What does this feel like? What are you doing to shift states?

Players will now have a pre-match image of the challenge state in their minds. Their match scripts will have given them specific instructions - you have managed them on an individual level (we will introduce a team script later in Soccer Brain). Now it's time for them to go out and physically work on the match script.

A Mental Wrapper

Most teams will start to physically warm up approximately 45 minutes to an hour before the game. This is their chance to experience their match script. This is their chance to put it into practice.

Insist that your players warm up in the style of their match script. You want to see it. You want to hear it. You want them to feel it.

If a player has a play within her match script to 'be vocal' then you want to see her being vocal. If a player has 'confident passes' then you want to see her pass with confidence. This is their opportunity to practice their match script before they play. This is their chance to sketch a blueprint of excellence on their mind.

It is during the warm-up that the match really starts to get going – not at kick-off. All too often I hear players tell me that the first 10 minutes is so important to them. They assert that this is the time they build momentum. Wrong! Momentum is built two hours before the game. Momentum continues to build into a player's warm up. This is when they should be getting 'mentally hot'. This is when their bodies and their minds should be attuning to high performance. This is when they want to dial in. At this time your role is to reinforce responsibilities and mindset through the medium of the match script.

Nothing and no-one takes you away from your match script. You make a mistake, you stay in the challenge state and you stay focused on your match script. Nothing and no-one takes you away from your match script.

Explode into the game by using your match script in your warm up. A physical AND mental warm up is required

During the Match – Playing in Trusting Mode

Inevitably players *do* shift into the threat state and they *do* forget their match script. That is football and that is what we all love about the game – it is unpredictable.

The great thing about your team members having match scripts is that you can, if you want, condense your on pitch communication into simple phrases - "Stick to your match script" or "Get back onto your match script" or "Focus on your match script" can be straightforward and effective messages.

In-match communication is a controversial subject matter. From speaking with many players at the top level of the game - most are indifferent. They claim to not hear what is being said or explain that they don't have the time to think about applying what has been said. They are, after all, trying to perform under pressure.

There is of course a counter argument. It is possible to convey something to your players during a game that can make a profound impact on the match. But it's important to keep things short and related to something you have worked on in training before. Players must be able to match what you are saying, with a picture in their mind, in as brief a period as possible. There can be no time for confusion.

However, to me the answer is simple: *train to trust on match day.*

Train skills, tactical awareness and understanding in your practice sessions. Do so thoroughly, so that you won't have to repeat yourself during a match. Then come game day - stand back and allow your players to compete. Give them the opportunity to shine. Screaming from the sidelines merely suggests that you haven't put the necessary work in during training.

For those who teach at the younger age groups I still believe this applies. Stand back. Let your young players play. They will make mistakes but that's okay. A game isn't the place to bark out orders – you'll only create panic and worry. Correct them in training and help them trust on match day.

It's unlikely that young footballers learn when you instruct during a game. Learning happens at a time when we are expecting a learning moment – when we are attuned to correction. On match day a young player should be let free to implement the tools, techniques and tactics that you have worked on with them during training. If you are concerned that you are missing a coaching opportunity, don't be – they are still learning. They are learning to do the right things in an environment of freedom. They are learning for themselves. If they continue to make the same mistakes you always have the post match debrief to deposit your thoughts on their soccer brain.

At older levels ignore the temptation to coach from the sidelines too much. An emphasis on match script is enough.

"Stay on top of your scripts. Focus on them. Let nothing and no-one take you away from them. If you shift to the threat state shift back to the challenge state as quickly as possible."

I believe a coach should have a couple of simple goals for herself on match day. They are quite simple:

Help your players play their match script and help them play the challenge state.

Is there really anything else you can do as a coach? As long as you lay down your tactics before the game that is all your responsibilities are. The result then takes care of itself.

Half Time

You may choose to dwell on a few tactical points but otherwise this is a great time to ask players to assess themselves on the match script and the challenge script so far. Do they think they're keeping great body language – are they BAMMING? Are they sticking to their script?

The half time team talk should never be too wordy or analytical because this may evoke confusion. You want them to stay in the challenge state. Bamboozling by bringing up new ideas should have health warnings attached to them. Occasionally something new may work, but most often such measures won't bring impact.

Allow your players a few minutes to settle and relax. A few minutes of peace and some time to breath helps the intelligent, front part of their brains switch on. It also allows you time to think about your feedback. But be careful – don't be tempted to comment too much. Questions are more powerful than statements at this time:

How can you improve upon your first half performance? What can you do to stay in the challenge state for longer? What helped you stay in the challenge state? What were your best moments in the first half that you want to continue doing in the 2nd half?

It's easy to make a statement related to the bad or to what *isn't* going well. And of course there should be time to remind players of your tactics, your plan of action, and what needs to go better from the first half. But asking the right questions can be so much more powerful. Opening up pictures of success, of excellence and of improvement is an alternative but effective approach to take in your half time team talk. It means less spoken words from you and a greater emphasis on *their* imagination.

Be different! Help players release a cocktail of chemicals that underpin an incredible performance – one full of confidence, focus and intensity. Ask the right questions. Immerse them in a world of their best and of their strengths. Help them *feel* great in preparation for the second half.

The Brain behind the Feet

As I stand on the sidelines within earshot of a coach I may be working with, I often find myself saying this:

"It's not the feet but the brain behind the feet."

A player constantly gives the ball away - "It's not the feet but the brain behind the feet." A player constantly finds herself out of position - "It's not the feet but the brain behind the feet." A player constantly allows a striker to get in front of him on a crossing ball - "It's not the feet but the brain behind the feet."

With a set of match scripts under your arm you can help your players manage their brain as they perform. The script helps them to play with fun, freedom and focus. It helps them settle their nerves before an intense fixture. It helps them play the challenge state. It helps in your communication with your team because it gives you something specific to communicate about. It helps them shift back into the challenge state if they dwell within the threat state. It helps you ask questions rather than make statements. It helps them trust. Match day is for trust.

In contrast it is on the training ground where they should be corrected most. It is on the training ground where they should do their serious thinking. It is the training ground where we head to next.

8

Practice on Purpose

Things weren't working out for Frank Rijkaard and his team. They were sluggish, lethargic and slow. They were second to the ball, and first runner up in the important games.

Their supporters weren't happy. The 9th of April 2008 saw their faithful jeer the side into a Champions League semi final as a result of continuous poor displays. That season they went on to finish second behind Real Madrid in the Spanish La Liga – a change was required.

That change came in the form of Pep Guardiola. A shift in personnel - perhaps one more important than the moment Lionel Messi signed for the club as a fresh faced eleven year old several years earlier. And indeed it was a turning point for the Catalan club who had fallen into the shadows of their main European rivals. Guardiola was quick to stamp his authority and leave a mark – a mark of excellence:

Xavi recalls the impact of the new manager's arrival: "We were just back from winning the Euros with Spain and instantly I could sense a different atmosphere, new standards and much more emphasis on getting fit. I recall saying to [Andres] Iniesta, 'We'd better hop on this train or it'll pass us by.'

"Standards had slipped. A kilo here or there didn't matter. A few minutes late here or there didn't matter. Now everything mattered. But Pep was right on top of everything like a hawk." Source: 442 Magazine "Inside the Mind of Pep Guardiola"

Standards are an important ingredient in your culture of commitment. It matters little what age group you work with, your coaching regime requires a benchmark of norms. These can be related to anything in your culture – being on time, work ethic, behaviour on the training ground, behaviour away from the training ground, protocols around match day. The list is endless.

But nothing is more important than the standards you have for yourself as a coach. Demanding the very best from yourself is an indispensable quality and a fundamental component of your coaching culture. You must strive to be at your very best at all times.

Pep Guardiola didn't care about the quality in front of him when he first arrived as coach of Barcelona. He didn't care that, on his first day on the training ground, standing in front of him were some of the best players in the world. All he cared about was helping those players to be the very best they could be.

Barcelona players in any generation are the epitome of talent (both physical and mindset). But Guardiola brought a different roadmap with him. It was his intention to nurture nature. He had to create a training regime that helped supercharge these footballing specimens to greatness. He had to create a team but he also had to get the very best from the individual talents that occupied the dressing room at Barcelona.

Individual Versus Team Training

There is a dilemma in the world of football coaching, especially at younger age groups. Teams and squads the world over, from under 6 through to elite first teams, contain individuals who need your personal attention. Every single soccer player requires the personal touch – they need to improve as team mates *and* as individual players. Yet how do you help players improve as individuals? How do you help your footballers grow as individual soccer players alongside improving them as a collective unit? Whilst many of your drills and exercises will help players develop individual technique and skill, this isn't enough. The quality of a player's soccer game is rarely judged during such training protocols. Opinions are formed on the pitch in games.

I believe this individual versus team training dichotomy can be seen at the very elite level of the game. Not enough is done to help individuals improve their game throughout their careers. I constantly hear of players in their early twenties who play in the world's top leagues being described as 'complete players'. No they aren't. No-one is ever a complete player – the game is too complex for that. Every soccer player should have a passion to learn no matter what their age, no matter what their level. Learning never stops. This isn't just a philosophical point. In science we are finding that it's a neurological fact.

The Learning Brain

The human brain never stops learning.

It was only until recently that researchers in neuroscience believed the brain was hardwired. They believed it was held constant across a person's lifespan. They thought that humans were fixed - attributes remaining constant and abilities preset and unchanging from birth.

We now know differently. Modern brain scanning equipment has shown that the brain changes. In fact it changes rapidly – every second of everyday. When we learn new information, whether facts or figures, or whether we carry out new motion or movement, the brain re-wires itself accordingly. The process is complex but the outcome is the same – we can all learn new skills and we can all learn to improve at whatever it is we want to develop. The brain is soft-wired *not* hardwired. The brain is malleable.

The soccer brain is changing all the time. The best coaches are the ones who tap into this brain plasticity. They find ways to help players change their neural networks quickly and effectively. The 21st century coach is one who builds on this by striving to help players become better learners. Yes, the onus is on *you* to help players understand and apply the information you provide for them - but an improved efficiency in a player's education process can be established when they become self-learners.

Hard work means nothing if it isn't correct work.
The same bad habits repeated in training will move
you away from your goal rather than toward

Focus of Attention

Have you stopped to consider that some of the best soccer players in the world aren't the most physically talented? Perhaps they are, in contrast to popular opinion, the best learners.

Much of my professional life in soccer has seen me in an observational role, standing to the side of the pitch, watching training. I'm fascinated by the interaction between coach and players and the impact this has on learning. A question I find myself asking is "Are these players learning?" The easiest thing for any coach to do is to regurgitate a series of exercises and drills. More difficult is to set the right learning environment and then ensure every player is fully focused on the words and actions the coach delivers. Focus is the operative word here. Learning requires an attentive mind – a mind that absorbs information.

Are your players fully focused when you are speaking or when you are demonstrating?

Don't brush over this question. A yes produces champions. A no slows and hinders development. If they are inattentive they're not listening. If they're not listening they won't understand. If they do not understand they're certainly not learning.

A coach needs learners who are deliberate in their thoughts and actions as they train. She requires learners who are self-aware and are able to think on the move. She needs intentional learners.

Intentional practice

This is *the* hot topic in sport coaching and sport psychology at the moment. Some call it deliberate practice others call it deep practice. I call it *intentional practice*.

Intentional practice is practice on purpose. It's training with improvement in mind. It's not just 'turning up to train and training'. And it's not just training hard! It's training with a series of goals in mind. It's training to improve weaknesses and magnify strengths. It's not necessarily training for perfection, but it *is* training for excellence.

There are four components of intentional practice – interesting, intense, internalised and integrated. Let's take a look at each one.

A relentless obsession with improvement must be the norm to the ambitious footballer

Interesting

Intentional practice is interesting. It captivates attention and holds it. It absorbs mindset. This doesn't mean that it's always fun, but it *is* meaningful to the individual in question.

Are you making your training sessions interesting? Are you including sessions that help players to stay alert, alive and switched on?

Interest mediates focus. The brain is constantly scanning the environment for stimuli to lock onto. That is how it has evolved. The brain will lock onto what it finds most attractive, what is most important to it in the moment. A footballer must find what he's working on significant to his game in order to focus his full attention on it.

This is why, a responsibility within your role as a coach, is to make sure the explanations of your drills and exercises are accurate and clear. It is *your* time to captivate attention. It is *your* time to sell your instruction.

Are you captivating the attention of your players before, during and after drills and exercises? Are you using the tonality of your voice to engage, to grip, to hold their gaze and open their minds? Are you using powerful words and simple explanation to help your players derive meaning from your sessions?

Attention starts the process of brain change. It starts the process of improvement.

Intense

Intentional practice is hard. It stretches you and pushes you out of your comfort zone. It demands more from you. It requires an inner voice that energises and shouts "push".

Are you helping your players stretch their comfort zone? Are you demanding more from them?

Intensity isn't just hard work. Intensity is also quality work. Intensity requires a soccer player to keep searching for excellence. If it's his body shape he is working on then he needs to maintain the discipline to keep the correct shape throughout training. If he is trying to take more shots in a game then he needs to break free from the habit of taking an extra touch or giving in to the temptation of passing the ball - and taking more shots no matter where he is on the park.

When a soccer player puts brain effort in (focused effort) he uses up a lot of glucose. It requires brain power – it can be exhausting. I often say to my players that after training physical tiredness should be nothing compared to the mental fatigue they feel. Brain effort is wearing on both mind and body. Intentional practice should be arduous.

Are you ensuring that players are putting focused effort into training? Are you insisting on mindset? Are you demanding focus? Are you demanding attention? Are you asking more from their brain resources?

Being driven is good...as long as it's in the right direction. Moving with speed must have direction - you must have quantity AND quality

Internalised

Intentional practice requires thought. It's not just action without judgement. That 'just do it' attitude and mindset is for match day. During training a player should be constantly examining the process of his practice:

- *"Am I keeping my body shape?"*
- *"Did I get into the right position like I wanted to?"*
- *"Have I taken more shots than yesterday?"*
- *"Am I timing my jumps on corners and free kicks better?"*

During intentional practice players are evaluating their performance as it unfolds. They are assessing their every action and every movement. They are aware of their performance. They have regular self check-ins that affirm how they are going; they are working hard enough or they are not, they are stretching their comfort zone or they are not, they are sticking to their goal process or they are not.

Are you asking your players to monitor themselves during training? Are you helping them become more self-aware?

Integrated

Just as players are self-aware during intentional practice they are also integrating their personal reflections with feedback from their coach.

Your feedback is a crucial determinant of their successful transition in the learning process. They can internalise and improve their awareness and understanding of their game but they can't see themselves play in the moment.

Is your voice reaching every player out there? Are you able to cast your expert eye onto every individual?

In a previous chapter I talked about insisting on mindset. Players also need your technical input. They need your observation of their form.

Feedback is crucial because it helps players feel a sense of certainty. It's not always immediately obvious to a player how she is performing. A striker who misses chance after chance may be performing well during build up play. She needs to know this. She needs to know the movement she has and the runs she's making are spot on. She needs to know the positions she's finding are helping her take the shots in the first place. She needs to know she's doing well. Her confidence relies on this type of feedback.

The ability to play positively under pressure doesn't happen overnight. It is a result of thinking correctly for 100's of training sessions

Accelerated learning: The Training Script

Your ability to immerse your players in intentional practice is greatly influenced by your communication before, during, and after training. However there is a technique to help them take greater responsibility for their training. It's called a training script.

Very similar to a match script, a training script helps players to practice with the four I's of intentional practice in mind. Simply, it demands players choose three things they are going to focus on and work on during the practice session. A defender's training script might look like this:

- *Improve timing up headers – eyes on man and ball to time correctly*
- *Practice keeping great body language at all times*
- *Practice communicating with my team mates – keep things positive (avoid negatives)*

The training script can relate to strengths a player wants to continue to magnify, as well as weaknesses they want to improve and should incorporate the four main components of performance – technical, tactical, mental and physical.

A midfielder's training script could look like this:

- *Improve first touch – focus on ball and play softly out of my feet*
- *Develop positioning awareness – constantly check my shoulders and scan for the right position. Play with position in mind.*
- *Make sure I'm on my toes at all times – enhance my focus*

You will have noticed that the plays in the training script are longer and more elaborate than those in the match script. This is necessary. The plays don't have to be catchy, but they *do* need to be thorough. Training is a time to critique and a time of thinking. It's a time of planning and development. A player must understand it's okay to think a little slower and be a bit more thoughtful during practice. It's a time of risk and a time of mistake.

A striker's training script might be:

- *Non-stop movement – pay attention to finding space. Never a lazy moment*
- *Have fun – I score when I enjoy myself*
- *Move into the 6 yard area rather than the front post – destroy that habit – get greedy for goals*

It is up to you how you introduce the training script to your players. For those coaches with little time why not ask your players to email you their scripts. By doing this you are asking them to take time to think about their strengths and weaknesses. You are asking them to become students of their game.

To improve their ability to complete a training script you can send them a list of the responsibilities within their role. Ask them to mark themselves out of 10 for each area. Ask them to be honest. Then if you have time, contribute a 'coach's mark'. If you don't have time to do this - simply work from their own judgement, their own mark. They should pick the lowest and the highest marks and look to focus on those areas. Players who seek to maintain strengths are ones who will retain confidence in their game – they will constantly fuel their feelings of certainty. But they also need to add areas of weakness into the mix. The training script is designed to pinpoint what needs to go better as well as what is already a picture of excellence.

A goalkeeper's training script could be:

- *Take my crosses more decisively – get that committed feeling as the ball is delivered*
- *Better vocals to defenders – not more but better*
- *Stay switched on when ball is down the other end of the pitch – use my body language – stay tall*

For you to be able to accomplish the final 'I' of intentional practice (integration) it is useful to keep a record of the plays in the training scripts of your players. By keeping a list of the scripts (or at least a mental note of them) you will be able to integrate your feedback with the execution of their scripts. You will be able to give accurate individual feedback – messages that are interesting to the player because they are meaningful. These messages can compliment, correct, or demand more. Through compliments and correction you can help players internalise with greater efficiency. By demanding more you can turn up the volume of their intensity.

9
Mental Contrasting

Many say he is the greatest Olympian ever.

It's no surprise. A typical training day in the diary of the 'Baltimore Bullet' was oriented to being the best. Get up at 6am. Swim for a couple of hours followed by gym. Something to eat, a sleep, then more working out. Day in, day out, he committed himself to this programme.

A structure for a champion maybe, but according to his long term coach it wasn't his rigorous training programme that set him apart from his peers. Nor was it his immense physique, the incredible support he garnered from his family or the club he trained at that was known for producing elite level swimmers. All those played a part but it was another component of performance that his mentor believed helped him win more gold medals than anyone else. According to swimming coach Bob Bowman, it was his psychology and his mindset.

The Psychology of a Champion

From the age of 12 Michael Phelps trained his mind. With the help of Bowman he exercised his confidence, his powers of focus, and his ability to imagine every day before, during, and after his swimming practice.

Bowman instructed Phelps on visualisation. He asked him to watch his 'personal videotape' before he went to sleep and just after he woke up. Of course this wasn't a real tape – it was an imagined movie formed in the mind of Phelps, one that helped him create a blueprint of success. Bowman had this to say about his then young charge:

"He's the best I've ever seen, and maybe the best ever in terms of visualisation. He will see it exactly - the perfect race. He will see it like he's sitting in the stands and he will see it like he's in the water."

But it wasn't just success that Phelps pictured. Bowman continues:

"He also spent time picturing things going wrong. The worst case scenarios."

Phelps would visualise his suit rip or his goggles fill with water.

"He would then have this picture in his database. He would have a set of solutions just in case a problem would arise during a swim meet. His nervous system would know what to do – it would be ready and prepared. He'll pick the one that is most suitable should he need to."

Such an approach may appear negative. It's easy to avoid doing such an exercise with soccer players. It's easy for a coach to think that this process will create some negativity amongst her players. This isn't true – not if you explain the task correctly. And before I do, let me tell you a little story as to how this exercise helped Phelps win one of his many gold medals.

*Play football with your eyes,
not your inner critic*

A Tale from Beijing

He knew there was a problem as soon as he hit the water. It was the Olympic Games in Beijing and this could have been a disastrous moment for him.

And after just a few metres the exact challenge he faced became apparent. Not only did he have a race to win against the finest swimmers in the world, he also had water leaking into his goggles.

It wasn't much at first but as the lengths passed so more water saturated the inside of the protectors that were supposed to shield his eyes from the water. He couldn't see! He couldn't see below him or in front of him. He didn't know where he was in the race – his location nor his position.

But he didn't panic.

He didn't panic because he'd been in this position before. Not literally of course, but mentally. He had spent many years planning for this eventuality. He had rehearsed it time and time again in the quiet of his bedroom – in the quiet of his mind.

As he turned into his last lap he calculated how many strokes his arms had to pump. It would be 20, maybe 21. He then started to count. His body remained perfect in its technique. He was relaxed but functioning at a high level of intensity. He soared through the water while he swam at full strength.

He could hear but he couldn't see. He could hear the roar from the crowd, but he was blind. They were urging him on but he had no idea he was the recipient of their encouragement.

As he neared the finish line he stretched out for one last surge, a final push. It was enough! He touched the wall before his rivals and as he removed the offending goggles, although his eyes stung from the water, he managed to glimpse the scoreboard. He was Olympic Champion with a new world record time.

He was asked afterwards what it was like to swim blind. His response was simple and eloquent:

"It felt like I imagined it would."

Expect to manage yourself on the pitch...
that is all you can expect

A Tale from an Old Client

My client imagined the worst as well – I wanted him to.

I asked West Ham striker Carlton Cole what it would look like if it all went wrong. I wanted him to think of such a scenario. This might sound strange given that, when Carlton first started working with me he struggled with his confidence levels. He tended to rehearse the negatives.

But midway into our relationship I felt like he had a more robust confidence and a better way of speaking to himself. He was able to take the positives from his training sessions and matches. He was able to look himself in the mirror and remind himself of his strengths as a striker. But he needed to grow further. He needed to become mentally stronger and have a more adaptable mindset during a match.

I remember the first time I asked Carlton the question "What are you going to do if it all goes wrong?" It was before a match against Derby County in the English Premier League. He was playing up front and was going to be marked by a big strong defender called Darren Moore. Carlton's physical presence was going to be compromised and he needed a plan B. So I asked him this question:

"If Darren Moore is on top of you for the first 10-15 minutes, if he 'owns' you, what are you going to do?"

I wanted Carlton to have a good think about the alternative strategies to playing up against a centre back, particularly a physically strong one.

Carlton's response was simple. He said he'd "Bring him in deep and pull him out wide." He said he'd use his movement to rid any of the momentum that Darren might have built up against him.

The fixture itself played out just as we had discussed. For the first 10 minutes Darren Moore was physically on top of Carlton. But Carlton recognised this and adjusted accordingly. He upped his work rate and became more adventurous with his movement. Rather than playing tight to Moore he tried to find space in different areas. He worked deep to link up with the midfield and to drag Moore into areas he shouldn't be in. Carlton also drifted out wide – if it wasn't going to be his day to score he could help one of his team mates to grab a goal by pulling his defender out of position.

The plan worked and West Ham won. Carlton didn't score but he gained 2 valuable assists for his club. Carlton was learning to become the complete player. He was learning thinking flexibility.

Picturing what can happen if it goes wrong isn't a negative moment – provided you mentally correct the scene it is more a moment of clarity

Thinking Flexibly

Thinking flexibly on the pitch is an important mindset skill for soccer players to develop. It's not easy. The game works at a frightening speed. There isn't much time to problem solve or to change a tactical approach. But it's an ability worth developing in your players.

Of course you *don't* want your players changing the game plan midway through the match. Tactics are your domain. But you *do* want players who are able to re-appraise when things go wrong. And you *do* want players who can adjust their approach if they are losing a personal battle against their opposite number.

Thinking flexibility and problem solving are products of thousands of hours of training. They are built through game knowledge and an understanding of solutions in context specific situations. The shape and pattern work you do on the training ground with your players will teach these most crucial competencies. The older player is at an advantage because he will have learned many ways to compete in his position.

But there is another way to learn and to work on thinking flexibility. It is a technique like the one Michael Phelps used as a teenage swimmer dreaming of taking on the world in the pool. And it is akin to the process I took Carlton Cole through – one that helped him think and play with intelligence under pressure.

A great coach sees failure as an education tool. A great player sees failure as a stepping stone to greatness

Mental Contrasting

Take your players through this process.

What will it look like if it goes wrong in the match on Saturday? What are you going to do as a striker if you are struggling to lose your marker? What are you going to do as a defender if momentum piles on top of you? What are you going to do as a midfielder if you're being marked out of the game? What are you going to do as a goalkeeper if you concede an early goal?

What does your plan B look like? What does it feel like?

Gabriele Oettingen is a professor at New York University and a global expert on self-regulation, goal setting and goal attainment. She has conducted a lot of research into the effects of thinking about what one wants to achieve. Through this research she discovered that an optimal strategy for setting any type of goal is to take time to think positively about the end goal while thinking realistically about what it will take to accomplish this. She calls this process mental contrasting.

Oettingen certainly didn't have soccer in mind when conducting her research but her findings hold true in sport. This is what Michael Phelps was doing when imagining worst case scenarios for his swimming meets. And this is what I helped Carlton to do before a football match.

It's not dissimilar to what double gold medallist Michael Johnson did in the build-up to his world record winning runs in the Atlanta Games of 1996. Johnson said that he spent up to half an hour a day visualising his performances – he envisioned success regularly. But Johnson also revealed that he included mental contrasting in his picture book. He would create an image in his mind of getting off to a poor start, having a poor first bend or trailing the leaders down the home straight. He would then strategise in his mind. He would take a little time to think about solutions – to think about being relaxed and clear minded in those situations.

Oettingen's mental contrasting technique can help your players. By asking them to be realistic about the process of performance you can help them strategise mentally and tactically. You can help them think about how they can turn around a personal battle being lost. You can build a series of pictures in their mind that paint solutions in a game being lost or a game where the opposition are on top. This process helps you help them become students of *the* game and students of *their* game.

If you're coaching very young players - give this a go with them. I believe in early exposure. Starting this form of questioning at 10 years old means your young players get to think about the nature of football and the challenges they face on the pitch. It helps them grow emotional toughness. It will help them cope with adversity as it strikes during a game. If they don't know the answer to your questions then provide a multiple choice set of answers, but make sure they are picturing the process of performance in their mind. Do this enough times and these pictures will linger. Eventually they'll stick.

Driving Your Culture of Commitment

Understand the difference between the challenge and threat states

Footballers respond in one of two ways to a match. When a player appraises the match in a positive manner he sees it as a challenge. When he appraises the match in a negative way he sees it as a threat. Get them in the challenge state!

Embrace Power Poses for yourself and for your team of players

Help their physiology drive their psychology. BAM their state – Body, Action, Movement. Incorporate power poses into their game. Help them act powerfully, think powerfully, and subsequently perform powerfully.

Use match scripts for all your players

Have your players write out several controllable goals related to their role within the match. These plays must be focused on what they want to achieve and towards mastery. Players must focus on their scripts from the warm up through to the end of the game.

Love to train the individual

Be passionate about coaching players individually as well as working on your team. Players require that personal touch no matter what their age or level. Tap the brain's ability to change and re-wire, and help your players become better self-learners.

Adopt and execute intentional practice in your training sessions

Intentional practice is practice on purpose. It's training with improvement in mind. It is training for excellence. There are four components – interesting, intensity, internalised, and integrated.

Ask your players to write training scripts

A training script helps players to practice with the four I's of intentional practice in mind. The script demands players choose three things they are going to focus on, and work on, during the practice session. Make them thorough!

Develop their ruthless streak through mental contrasting

Many leading athletes take time to picture what might go wrong during a game. This isn't negative. It helps them to strategise what they'll do given that scenario. Ask players to picture dealing with the problems that may arise in a match.

Section Four
A Culture of Cohesion

You, the coach, are integral to the cohesion your team demonstrates on and off the pitch. Through your actions, your attitude, and your voice, you shape your players' feelings of cohesion – on the training pitch, at home (away from the pressures of training) and under the lights on match day.

As a coach you must help your players feel cohesive – together, us, bonded, in unison, collaborating, joined – a collective.

Soccer is as much an individual sport as it is a team sport – individuals want to do well for themselves. You, the coach, have to team them as individuals. When they trust you and are on your side you have to build cohesion. You have to help them see what their teammates see. You have to help them think what their teammates think. A shared prediction of play is the optimal group mindset. Minds absorbed in the moment, working as one.

As a coach you must care about the 'me' before you turn all of the 'me's' into 'we'. When players see that you are thoughtful of them as people *and* as players - then they will team for you.

A team needs a leader. One who has a vision, a plan, an approach and one who forces the execution of strategy. A team needs a leader. One who inspires and helps players to aspire. A team needs a leader. One who promotes fun, freedom and focus. One who guides them on their journey through good times and bad.

As a coach you need to be a leader. You need a road map, a mental compass and a mindset tool kit to manage your people and players. But before you can lead others, you must lead yourself. Before you can direct others, you must direct yourself. Self-awareness and self-development are the leader's rod and staff.

This next section in Soccer Brain introduces you to a blueprint that holds the keys to implementing a culture of cohesion. The formula is simple:

1. SHOW Leadership
2. Reflect through different lenses
3. Think the 'me' before the 'we'
4. Develop a power plan
5. Build the pelican mindset
6. Script your team
7. Stereotype your team

10
Leading with Head and with Heart

'3 years of excuses and it's still crap. Ta ra Fergie!'

That message was unfurled on the terraces of the Stretford End – the west stand and spiritual home of the Manchester United supporters. Old Trafford, the Theatre of Dreams, December 1989 – a famous club in crisis.

Fans were frustrated at the month's results - losses against Crystal Palace, Arsenal, Spurs and Aston Villa didn't help the mood, while the team was only good enough for a draw against Wimbledon and Arsenal. Things had to change, and change quickly.

A few days into a new decade a determined coach stood on the sidelines as he watched his United side take on Nottingham Forest in the third round of the world's oldest domestic knockout tournament – the FA Cup. His beleaguered players had to win; his job was on the line, his career in tatters if they were to exit the competition that day.

The goal that, many say, saved Sir Alex Ferguson was as industrious as any scored by a United team over the past 25 years and perhaps a glimpse at the type of team goals that were awaiting their supporters. The lively Lee Martin pressed and tackled Forest midfielder Toddy Orlygsson and then played a short pass to Mark 'Sparky' Hughes. Hughes took one look up and noticed his strike partner,

Mark Robins, on the edge of the box. Sparky then played an inch perfect pass around the back of the Forest defenders with the outside of his boot. The ball gently curved left to right on the ideal trajectory and on the perfect height for Robins to attack. With the help of a shove in the back by Forest defender Stuart Pearce, and a gentle nod of the head, Robins was able to ease the ball beyond the flailing arms of goalkeeper Steve Sutton and see it nestle in the back of the net. The cup tie was won.

With that victory momentum switched in United's favour and they went on to lift the FA Cup that year. The rest is history.

A Different Viewpoint

I don't think Sir Alex Ferguson's career was saved by Mark Robins' goal. 'That goal' could have been scored a week later or a month later. 'That goal' could similarly have been 'that save' or 'that tackle' or 'that pass'. Soccer matches are determined by small moments of truth – Mark Robins' close range effort was one of many flashes of skill on show during the game that impacted the result.

More pertinent than the game against Forest was the perception and opinion the Manchester United hierarchy had of Ferguson. They refused to look at results – they ignored three years without a trophy. They were able to do this because they saw the leadership qualities the greatest of all modern managers displayed. If the United board felt that Ferguson's leadership had divided a dressing room, that his tactics were misplaced, or that his leadership was building a weak organisational culture, they would have terminated his contract with immediate effect. But they saw what fans couldn't necessarily see. A man with vision and a man hell bent on doing everything he could to build a winning culture and a winning team packed full of world class individuals. He just needed time. And his leadership talent enabled his superiors to give him just that. He had been given a chance to SHOW his leadership.

SHOW Leadership

To build your culture of cohesion you must SHOW leadership. Cohesion within a team or a soccer organisation is impossible without great leadership. SHOW is an acronym I use when I sit down with a coach who wants to improve her leadership skills. If she's looking for a few simple pointers to help her deal with the people and player challenges she faces within her club or soccer organisation then this model can SHOW her how.

- S in SHOW stands for servant. A soccer coach must be a servant to her players and people.
- H stands for host. A soccer coach must be an accomplished host.
- O stands for optimism. A soccer coach must lead through optimism in good times and bad.
- And finally, W stands for will. A soccer coach must be wilful of heart and of mind.

Let's take a closer look at the philosophies underpinning the SHOW leadership model.

It's the space in-between the player & the coach that counts, the communication

Servant

A great leader is a servant. This may sound strange. A servant is seen as subservient but the leader is seen as the man or woman 'out front'. A servant is obedient and compliant yet it is the leader who is responsible for attitude and action, setting out and asserting the rules of engagement.

There are of course many differences between the roles of servant and leader but there are similarities too. To lead is to be passionate about helping. A great leader is 'help served on a plate'. He is there to assist, support and facilitate – just like a servant. He is there to make the life of his subordinates easier. He is there to listen, to show empathy and be attentive to the needs of others.

The soccer leader is a *servant* to his players, his team and his club. There are a set of criteria related to this role – a collection of responsibilities, attitudes and behaviours that help you play servant.

Detail: The servant is a details man (or woman). He leaves no stone left unturned to deliver the best possible service he can. His work is carried out with an eye for excellence. Nothing is taken for granted. He checks fact and introduces new, more efficient ways to progress. He looks for the 1% nudges.

You as coach *must* sweat the details. Your planning must take an exact look at the minutiae. You must project yourself into the future and think of every eventuality and plan accordingly.

Are you focusing on the small things – the areas of development and performance that often get overlooked? Are you looking in detail at tactics? Are you sweating the individual mindsets of your players?

Are you striving to do what others can't be bothered to do? It's not just about having the perfect session plan it's about how you communicate that plan. It's not just about having what you believe to be the correct tactics for a match – it's about having a plan B, as backup, if it goes wrong.

If you are not great on detail then you certainly need to delegate this to someone. You need a right hand man who will hold the microscope against the behaviours of your coaching culture. You need a details person by your side to cross the t's and dot the i's.

Listen: The servant is a great listener. He has to be otherwise he'd never acquire the information required to carry out his duties. He not only listens, he hears. He determines exact details from the messages of his master so he can act accordingly.

You as coach *must* listen. When a player comes to you with doubt or with fear you must listen without prejudice. You must hear what a player or a parent or an official has to say. Listening is the foundation of great relationships. And without a relationship you cannot build trust.

Are you listening to your players? Are you building their trust through deliberate listening? Can they see that you care – that you are paying attention to their challenges?

At times you must listen without commenting. This is tough – we are conditioned to react or to comment when others speak. But if you wait and listen you will get to hear the whole story. You will get to see the whole picture.

You must listen with an open mind. You must listen to the *feeling* behind the words and sentences. A servant truly focuses on his master - you should truly focus on your players. Avoid just stepping in. A silent coach is a listening coach.

Great leaders in business are such because they listen (and hear) what the customer wants - enabling them to provide a suitable and sellable product. In coaching, listening aids solution. Resolution can only be found if you know where the problem lies. Listen to your people and you will help them improve more than they ever thought they could.

Adapt: The servant is adaptable. He will change according to the needs of his master. He will shift his behaviour if the master requires it or if his work isn't being received as he would want it to.

You as coach *must* be adaptable. Stubbornness with tactical or leadership approaches won't work. A flexibility for change is a must with its facilitation at the right moment. If things aren't working then humility and a willingness to adapt are the considered approaches.

Are you able to look in the mirror and accept that the weight of evidence suggests what you are doing isn't working? Can you change direction? Are you robust enough?

Adapt slowly. A lost game shouldn't necessarily mean the reorganisation of a team. Slow, small shifts may be conservative but it's important not to be rash. A poor game shouldn't mean the end of your relationship with a player. A poor training session shouldn't mean you dismiss a player's ability. But some movement in behaviour may be required.

Always be honest with yourself and others. Always accept that, in your position as coach, things will inevitably go wrong. Be open-minded with change. Believe in your systems and processes but always look to update them with new formulas and new ideas. The best coaches adapt when they need to.

Over-deliver: The servant over-delivers. He provides for his master time and time again, always throwing himself into his task. The very best servants know their masters so well they will pre-empt their needs. They will surprise and delight their master by under-promising and over-delivering.

You as coach must over-deliver. Your students and your players are your masters. You must give them all they need to be the best they can be. Deliver on deep satisfaction. Be earlier than on time and always be set up. Stay later to talk with players or parents or auxiliary staff.

Over-delivering doesn't mean over-analysis or providing players with too much information. You don't want to confuse them. But it does mean being present as often as you can be. It does mean having a mind on them rather than yourself.

Do this. Have a mind on them. Over-commit yourself to helping. In this way your leadership will build your team.

Are you over-delivering for your team and your people within your soccer organisation? Do you surprise and delight your players. Is there loyalty to you? Is your loyalty infectious? Do you care more for them than they care about themselves?

The will to win is shadowed by the will to prepare & learn

Host

A great leader is a host. We've all hosted a party. We've all been in that hot seat where we have to entertain our guests. A host has to make sure his guests are having a great time. He has to ensure they're meeting new people, they're being well fed and he has to make certain their glass is constantly being topped up. It's a time when the introverted have to break free from the shackles of social timidity and embrace the outer world. A host is outgoing, relaxed in company, approaches people, and is approachable.

Is this any different to your role as a coach? You have to make sure that your players are focused in training, are working together as a team and are staying confident. Depending on your coaching position you have to manage relationships with parents, officials and the club hierarchy. You have to stand at the front, speak, and enjoy delivering instruction. You are in the spotlight and your behaviours must align with this position.

The soccer leader is a *host* of his players, his team and his club. There are a set of criteria related to this role – a collection of responsibilities, attitudes and behaviours that help you play host.

Care: The host of a party minds his guests. He doesn't ignore, snub or turn his back. He is responsive to the needs of his party goers. Everyone counts. He wants everyone to have a great time and takes it upon himself to make sure this happens.

You as coach *must* care. Every player is important and significant. If you work with young players then every parent counts (no matter how challenging they may be). Your club officials may not know the game like you but your standards must not wane – you must care for them too.

To care is to appreciate that every player, whatever their age or standard, is as human as you are. Every player has needs and wants and doubts and fears just as you do. Cold shouldering or being impatient is to go against what it is to be a coach.

Captivate: The host of a party has to hold the interest of his guests. He has to circle the room going from guest to guest and group to group starting conversations, joking, telling stories, introducing topics, asking questions and asserting opinions. The best hosts enthral, fascinate, and mesmerize.

You as coach *must* captivate. You must hold the attention of your players. Through your words you must inspire and you must help them to aspire. Sir Alex Ferguson captivated. He had a vision and found the players he wanted to take with him on that journey. Paul Scholes shared this end in mind. As did David Beckham, Gary Neville, and Ryan Giggs. They were captivated. They were enthralled.

Lead your people by captivating them. Share your vision, your destination with them and sell the process. Use emotive words, find the inspirational sentence. Show off an exciting picture and they'll follow you.

Approachable: The host of a party has to be approachable. He has to attend to his guests and listen closely and carefully. Perhaps they want something to make them feel more comfortable or perhaps they just want the host's attention. Either way, the host is at the hub of the party and he must open himself to contact.

You as coach *must* be approachable. You must display open body language, a smile and friendly gestures. You must be prepared for conversation. If it's a time that is inconvenient ask the player, parent, or member of staff, if it would be okay to speak with them at a time when you can give them your full attention. If you can't focus on them you can't lead them.

Take a few minutes to cast your mind back to the last few sessions you've given. Have you been approachable? Did your body language say "I care"?

Team: The host of a party brings people together. He helps them find common ground – shared interests and interesting conversation. At the beginning of the party his guests may have been strangers. But as the party develops strangers become friends, perhaps only for the duration of the gathering but that's all that counts to the host.

You as coach *must* team your players and your people. They have one thing in common – soccer, but this is where their similarities will end. They will have different needs and wants. Perhaps they have different motivations, hopes and expectations. Harmony and cohesion are delivered in football by collective mindsets – ones that are focused on the task at hand. Your players and your people should immerse themselves in the task that is laid out to achieve the desired outcome. It is *your* job to help them do that. It is your job to pull people together, to stay on task, in every training session in every game.

A slice of social cohesion helps. Players who like each other will pull together more easily. But 'liking' is not necessarily linked to improvement or winning. Task cohesion has stronger links to team success than social solidity. We will discuss this further in the next two chapters.

The coach as leader helps players feel special by bringing them together, by caring, by showing interest and by driving them to succeed

Optimist

A great leader is an optimist. She sees the future and believes it is possible to get there. She envisions great things – achievement, success, and victory. She says "can" when others say "can't". She says "how can I" when others say "no way". She says "What *is* possible?" when others say "It is not possible."

Scientists believe that optimism is 50% hereditary. This leaves a mammoth 50% that can be developed, improved upon, and built. It leaves the door open for *you* to become an optimistic leader. It suggests that you can lead with your voice and with your attitude. It hints that you can inspire and help others aspire.

The soccer leader is someone who demonstrates an attitude of optimism with all things related to her players, her team and her club. She believes her players can be the best. She believes they can win. She believes that, when adversity strikes, the solution is in front of her or just around the corner.

The optimistic leader in soccer is more successful than the pessimistic one because such a trait develops strength in the face of tough times. It enhances motivation when all appears lost. It builds confidence and focus. It projects itself onto others and bestows these qualities onto them as well. There are a set of criteria related to this role – a collection of responsibilities, attitudes and behaviours that help you become the optimistic leader.

Passion: The optimistic leader is passionate. She believes in her charges no matter who they are or where they have come from. She exposes strengths and empowers. She cajoles and stretches.

As coach you *must* be passionate. Enthusiasm and love for the game must be apparent not only in your body language but in your words, in your sentences and in all your communication with your players.

Your players can see it. They can see the passionate or the passionless. Your words and motion give it away. With passion you inspire. With passion you give permission for players to love the game as much as you do.

Big picture: The optimistic leader sees the big picture. Have you ever heard of the recency effect? This is a phenomenon that most of us adhere to. It is a psychological term that relates to the fact that one is more likely to remember ones most recent experiences and will continue to do so into the future. So, for example, if on a car journey you see an equal number of blue and green cars, but see a whole bunch of blue cars towards the end of your travels, you are more likely to believe there were more blue cars along the way. The optimistic leader is able to look beyond the recent and remind everyone of the big picture – the objective being strived for.

You the coach *must* see the big picture. Big picture thinkers learn without judgment. A loss here, a loss there doesn't trigger an emotional overwhelm. Losses don't predict the future for optimistic soccer coaches, they merely inform the future. Equally, the big picture thinker doesn't allow an overdose of positive emotion to invade her mind when she wins. It is only a win!

Are you, as leader, managing your emotion? Are you seeing the big picture after training? The performance of a player in a single session won't determine her trajectory – be calm, coach her and help her – don't berate her. Likewise, a single game doesn't make a season. A single match doesn't lose a Championship, nor does it win one either. Be calm, be patient. See the big picture.

Energy: An optimist releases energy in others. He helps others recognise their strengths. He looks for hidden potential and helps his charges believe that they can. An optimist is a strong communicator – you cannot release energy in others unless you have an ability to communicate a message with fervent enthusiasm.

You the coach *must* have energy and be an energiser. As a soccer coach every word you say counts. Every sentence you speak counts. I am passionate about the value of words and their impact on the energy of players, a team and their performance. You must be too.

Your body must exude energy during a training session. You require your players to compete with energy then why not you too? Your external behaviour is a window into your internal thoughts. Great soccer leaders have a deep internal passion for their sport, for learning and for performance.

In his book, "It Worked for Me", the American politician Colin Powell, told how the following was drilled into him when he was in the army: "Lieutenant, you may be starving, but you must never show hunger. You may be freezing or near heat exhaustion, but you must never show that you are cold or hot. You may be terrified, but you must never show fear. You are the leader and the troops will reflect your emotions." Quite simply leadership is about maintaining energy levels, yours and those of your players, no matter what is happening in training and no matter what is happening as they compete. You are their rock. You are their energiser.

Risk: The optimistic leader takes risks. She goes against the grain, against the flow of the world around her. The risk taker goes a different way to the normal path at times. You must take this route as coach on occasion. Most love the status quo. Not the optimistic leader. She looks to the left when others look to the right. She finds a new way.

As coach you *must* be a risk taker. You must empower others to take risks. You must promote freedom and help players practice the art of carefree abandon under pressure. There can be no glory in safety. There can be no glory in chains. Give yourself and your players the freedom to make mistakes. Give yourself and your players permission to concede goals. You'll find you'll keep more clean sheets!

Let your players use their agility. Let them take players on. Let them deliver an extraordinary performance full of flair and ambition and courage. When you win in this style - celebrate. When players learn new skills - celebrate. Find fun in the power of risk taking.

Find new formulas. Find new methodologies. Coaches should never stand still. Borrow from the past but fix your eyes firmly on the future. Never forget there is a world full of information that will enhance your current practices. Go searching for it. Do things the new way. Take risks.

Let your players off the leash. Then your players will play with fun, freedom, focus, looseness, and confidence. Your players will invent. Your players will express themselves. Your players will take risks under pressure.

Influence the risks your players take by being an optimist. They can do it — tell them they can!

Will

A great leader shows will - a will to succeed, a will for others to succeed, a will to learn, a will to develop, a will to perform and a will to sustain. A great leader sustains this - through good times and bad. She sustains discipline in herself and others no matter what the outcome. Having the will of a leader is to discover self-reliance, to acquire the stamina to persevere, and to develop the vital qualities necessary for success.

A soccer leader requires will. He needs a strong mind when his team loses – he cannot afford to be emotionally engulfed. Taking an objective viewpoint into soccer matches is critical for sound judgement tactically and important for rational communication with players.

There are a set of criteria related to this role – a collection of responsibilities, attitudes and behaviours that help you become a leader with will.

Desire: Leaders with will have desire. They have a vision, a dream, and they move heaven and earth to accomplish this end goal. The image that their mind houses - drives them every single day.

As coach you *must* show desire. But it is where you direct this desire that is important.

Your desire must centre on your players. You must want them to be the very best they can be, as individuals and as team mates. Desire as a soccer coach means development. It means being passionate about providing a platform for learning. Desire in coaching relates to having a passion and a love for seeing players improve.

Do you love to see your players improve? Do you show them this? Do you tell them this?

Desire is also about winning, specifically doing the things you and your players have to do to win. Desire in football is about loving the detail behind the victory, not just the outcome itself.

People confuse desire. They think it's the fist pumping on the side of the pitch. They think it's shouting at players. They think it's instructing loudly in that final five minutes. They actually think desire is seen on match day. This is a long way from the truth. Desire is demonstrated on the training field long before anyone steps under the lights to play their game. Desire is demonstrated in the quiet times in the video analysis room. Desire is demonstrated with your head in books. Desire is demonstrated in a continuing professional development course. That is true, lasting desire.

Dedication: Leaders with will are dedicated. They are committed to the cause. They sweat the small stuff. They spend much of their social time mentally rehearsing their work.

As a coach you *must* be dedicated. You must work harder and better than other coaches. You must have a passion to improve yourself to help you improve others.

Dedication means the last to turn off the lights. Dedication is scouting the opposition games on a cold and wet Wednesday evening. Dedication is driving to see someone who can give you a couple of clues as to how you can get better.

Are you a dedicated coach? Are you exhausting every avenue for success?

A coach who is truly dedicated never loses sight of her goal. And what is her goal? To improve her players and win more games. Her goal is to supply her players with the tools to succeed, to deliver success.

Sir Alex Ferguson was as dedicated a manager as you will find. His life revolved around football. Daily training, match preparation and managing players - young and old - consumed him. As did dealing with agents, the press, and his back room staff. His eye was always cast on soccer. He kept himself updated with the latest goings on in the world game. His success was not a product of those famous match days at Old Trafford where the fans in the Stretford End would sing his name across 20 years. His success came *away* from the public view during those quiet times of management and study. Perhaps this is why he had a special love for players such as Eric Cantona, who chose to practice beyond the normal designated training times. He loved his commitment. He appreciated his dedication.

Discipline: Leaders with will are disciplined. Ultimately the most crucial component of leadership might well come down to managing oneself. If a leader can manage himself then he can manage his people. If he can inspire himself then he can inspire his people. If he can motivate himself then he can motivate his people.

As a coach you *must* be disciplined. A disciplined coach has a better chance of developing disciplined players. Great leadership spreads by its own positive energy. Through self-leadership we exude great habits onto others.

My bottom line is simple. Great coaches don't accept mediocrity - they constantly seek improvement in themselves and others. They bring discipline to every area of their life, and strive to help their players bring discipline to theirs.

Do you bring discipline to the games of your players? Do you have the same standards for yourself as you do your players? Can you expect them to stay disciplined in their team shape if they don't have discipline in their everyday lives? Can you expect your striker to score 30 plus goals per season if she doesn't have the discipline to put in the extra hours or the discipline to engage in intentional practice?

Determination: Leaders with will are determined. They work hard, stick at it and believe in what they are doing. They have the stomach to fight hard through adversity.

As a coach you *must* be determined. You must stick to things until you win the battle. You must possess a will, a driving force and an awesome power.

You lose, you push forward. You draw, you push forward. Your best player leaves you, you push forward. A parent has a go at you, you push forward. Other people don't believe in you, you push forward.

Nothing can stop you and no-one can tell you to stop. You must lead yourself every single day. You must be the best you can be in every single training session. Nothing can stop you and no-one can tell you to stop.

Be ambitious and be relentless. Keep moving forward. Keep developing. Keep learning. Keep improving others. Obsess the detail. Prepare thoroughly. Be better than others. Be the best you.

Love to lead others. Show desire. Lead them with determination and keep moving forward no matter what

The best leaders

Are there any qualities that I have listed that the great Sir Alex Ferguson didn't have in his leadership armoury? His success was due to his complete leadership.

He didn't help produce some of the finest British players because of his infamous temper. He succeeded in spite of his famous "hairdryer" treatment. He won more trophies than any manager in the modern era because he was able to develop players individually and collectively. He was able to sell a vision and inspire a team to work their backsides off to achieve his goals for his organisation.

Reflection

During Sir Alex's 26 years as manager of Manchester United the game of soccer changed dramatically in England. The English Premier League was formed in the early 1990's and gave rise to the most powerful league in world football. Competition to win the title grew stronger as players from all over the world looked to move to England and compete in the toughest and best paid league. Ferguson managed to re-build winning team after winning team. He fought off competition from Blackburn then Arsenal, Chelsea and latterly Manchester City.

His 26 years saw an advance in sport science. The Scottish manager had to get to grips with training protocols that would have been other-worldly back in his playing days and formative coaching years in the 1970's. But he was able to adapt. He was able to examine a new idea, a new science, or a new coaching methodology and introduce it into his armoury if he felt it appropriate. He was also able to constantly improve himself. He never stood still – he was constantly changing, improving and developing.

This flexibility was a product of his ability to scrutinise his own leadership. A strength of his was the ability to reflect on his actions and answer honestly and humbly whether the reactions he was getting were useful, promoted development and teamship, and encouraged growth within the Manchester United organisation.

As a soccer leader you need to develop the capacity to reflect. Reflection is a meaningful way for you to gain genuine understanding of yourself and others within your club and organisation. It can be uncomfortable, but in its absence there is a constant risk of poor decisions, maladaptive coaching behaviour and bad judgements.

'Know thyself' may be the quickest route to leadership success

Your Leadership Lenses

Who are the people who make up your soccer organisation? Even if you are just a one man band there are more than just you and your players. In youth soccer there are the players and their parents or guardians. For adult soccer there are partners, husbands and wives. In big soccer organisations there are your fellow coaches, your board of directors, your auxiliary staff such as sport scientists, physios, volunteer workers (oh, and sport psychologists!).

A key skill in developing your ability to reflect on your leadership actions, attitudes and decisions is to imagine yourself into the minds of the people who are affected by your leadership processes. Adopt their viewpoint. See the world through their eyes, through their lenses. There are several lenses to take:

Your own: Write a coaching journal and include the reaction and responses you receive from your actions and communication. Write about your frustrations and successes. What is fuelling them? What do you do that helps people react well to you and to your instruction? Examining your thoughts and feelings about your journey enables you to reflect on your activities and adjust accordingly.

Your players and families: How do your followers see you? When you walk into a room what are they thinking? How do their families perceive you and your leadership style? A thorough reflection requires a knowledge of how those who are subordinate to you see you. Such an examination builds cohesion – a shared vision. Questions to be asked include: Are you being too controlling? Are you managing them enough? Are you engaging critical others including parents and partners? Are you caring enough for them? Are you showing this in the form of attention? There are hundreds of questions you can ask yourself with relation to the perception of others of your leadership.

Your colleagues: A third lens focuses on those you work alongside. They may be your superiors, on your level, or below you in the coaching chain. How do they see you as a leader? How do they go about their leadership process? How do they lead others? These questions can help you have a critical conversation with yourself that helps you examine different viewpoints and differing leadership styles. Leaders who are able to detach from their own leadership style, and ways of doing, develop their ability to be more robust in the face of adversity, conflict and different player personalities. They learn to adjust according to the situation they confront. It is advisable to talk to other leaders in your organisation regularly. Get their point of view. Shared information with colleagues leads to better recognition and definition of problems, improved lines of communication and increased decision-making effectiveness.

The effective leader is one who leads through relationships with others by managing his interactions, his treatment of players, how he provides feedback, and how he deals with conflict. Tuning into leadership behaviours as a coach helps improve relationships and it is the leader's lenses that aid this process. In turn this reflection helps the coach build on his ability to SHOW leadership on and off the pitch. Now let's look a little closer at the intricacies of bonding your players.

11
We Starts with Me

"Call me!"

These were the last audible words from the 'Special One' as coach of the then Champions of Europe. As he climbed into the car he was already preparing himself for a new challenge.

But as he got himself comfortable in the back seat of his drive, emotion overcame him and he instructed his chauffer to stop. The car had travelled no more than 20 metres. Without hesitation, perhaps without thought, he got back out and made for the downcast player whom he had directed his last instruction to.

With every step toward the player the Special One's eyes filled with tears. He was moving on and once again leaving behind players he'd grown to love. His easy charm, his grit, his confidence, had always hidden other more complex aspects of his emotion. But you can't be a great coach without a range of emotion. And you can't be a great coach without attachment to your players – your warriors – the ones who win and lose for you, the ones who affirm or deny your greatness.

The player standing to the side of the road was Marco Materazzi. An Italian pit bull, hero to some, villain to others - the Special One had used him sparingly and sensibly in the twilight of his career. They had a relationship – a strong bond. Materazzi: the Inter mascot, the player the Special One could lean on for cheerleading and goading the opposition.

The Special One hooked his right hand around the neck of Materazzi and wrenched him into a hug. As they embraced for a final time both player and manager wept. This final goodbye, a sign of what had come before – loyalty, pride, honour, discipline, respect, desire and pure passion. World class coaching for world class players. Jose Mourinho, a very special coach indeed.

The I in Win

Mourinho is special because he is, by and large, able to get the very best out of the individual players he works with. And this helps him team them.

Teaming is important. Teams win championships. Players *must* team. If you're a coach developing very young players then teaching them how to play within a team will be a part of your everyday coaching process. But players *must* be great individuals as well great teammates. They must be nurtured in a culture that allows them to express themselves as individuals.

Team building starts with the understanding that your job as coach is to help players be the very best individuals they can be. Soccer is still an individual sport. Individuals win games. Individual performance is critical to outcome. Individual toughness heavily influences result.

- *Without an individual moving into space there is no-one to pass to*
- *Without an individual losing his marker there is no-one to cross to*
- *Without the individual goalkeeper making great saves you can't win*
- *Without an individual defender clearing off the line or winning headers you can't keep a clean sheet*
- *Without an individual striker finding the space to tap home from five yards out you may not have scored*
- *Without the talented individual midfielder looking up and spotting the pass that led to a goal you may have lost rather than drawn*

Every week matches are won or drawn because individuals do something great – for themselves and for their teammates. Similarly, individuals let down their teams and themselves. Individual errors are often the costly mediator of a match.

At the heart of Championship teams are great individuals who perform under pressure but who are willing to team when they train and when they perform. It is your job as coach to give them a reason to team with others. You have to give them that all important feeling of cohesion. You have to get them on your side.

Allow individuals to be themselves — make them feel special — and they'll team up for you

Getting them Onside

Players won't team for you if they don't see a reason to. You have to build trust and loyalty.

To garner trust you've got to show that you care. You've got to show that you, as leader, will take the bullet. And you've got to add to their game. This isn't the same as changing their play. Imparting your knowledge requires a subtle touch - blending old and new. What are they good at already? Tell them. What can they add? Tell them. Let's explore this in more detail.

Care for Them

It is rare for leaders, no matter what their industry, to be both liked and respected. I guess they are to be found but it's difficult to be liked by everyone against a backdrop of tough day-to-day decisions to be made.

You don't have to be liked or respected to team a group of individuals but it helps if you care about them. If you care for the players you may become liked. If you care for the games of the players you may become respected. If you care for both the person behind the play *and* the game that makes the plays then you may become liked *and* respected. But perhaps most importantly of all - you can help team the group of individuals you have in front of you.

Caring about the individual gives him less excuse to act as one and more reason to work cohesively with others in his squad. In my experience individual problems arise when members feel they are being ignored or neglected.

Care about your players. If they are young learn about their challenges at school. If they are an adult learn about their family. What are their hobbies outside of soccer? What music do they like? What films have they recently seen? Taking the personal touch with a player will make it harder for him to feel ostracised if something happens that he doesn't like. It will make it tougher for him to moan and groan at colleagues at a decision you make that he feels is wrong. It will make it harder for him to start an undercurrent of blame or problem-making or excuses.

Care about your players. Fall in love with their individual games. Strive to know their games better than they know their games. Know what they do when they do it well, and know what they do when they are at their worst. An understanding of the performances of your individual players gives them certainty that you are the coach to help them.

If you care for the person and his game do you think he will bitch and whinge about you? Do you think he'll harm team spirit or togetherness?

The key to caring is simple. Show an interest. Get involved. Be engaged in the challenges a player faces on and off the pitch. Express concern at problems but be optimistic about solutions. Help the player. Extract from them the specifics of the situation and offer ideas. I've never worked with a client who has said to me "The coaching staff care too much for me. They are really easy to speak to, and I don't like that." I don't think I'll ever have that kind of conversation with a player.

You can never care too much as far as I'm concerned. All too often I work with players who tell me they are ignored by coaches. They tell me there is a lack of empathy from those who are supposed to be helping them.

Practice being interested. Improve your ability to understand others' needs by arriving for training with a goal to speak to as many individuals as possible. Practice open body language. Practice being engaged in conversation with a player. Get them on your side.

Take the Blame

I'm sure it will come as no surprise if I were to say that I cringe when I watch a coach blaming a player for a defeat or pointing out the poor performance of a single player.

It's never a player's fault. Your players as individuals and as team mates are merely a reflection of your coaching. Never blame a player in public. Never speak ill of a player behind his back. If correction is required then do so in private with a player. Be honest and be open. Being transparent with players builds trust and subsequently builds winning teams.

If your team wins it's "us". If your team loses it's "I". Be committed to this process. Avoid the temptation to make an excuse or point fingers away from yours. This doesn't mean you should be beating yourself up if your team loses or if a player has a disastrous game. But self-acknowledgement will not only help you develop yourself as a coach – it will also go a long way to helping you develop a team out of a bunch of individuals.

This also doesn't mean that you ignore tactical correction after a lost game. You may point to yourself in private and outside of the changing room. But inside you must be open and honest with your players. If a player has made a mistake point the error out and tell him what he needs to do better next time. There is no need to shout the place down, but there is need to align the player's mind with the play he should have made. But your communication to the outside world must involve the 'we'.

A coach spends himself in a worthy cause if he always sees himself at fault. It is never the player it is only the coach

Feedback

I have walked into coaching cultures in football clubs where feedback has been sparse. Coaches haven't spoken to some of their players – sometimes for weeks. Many coaches don't inform players that they won't be playing in the next game. Some coaches don't have any form of systematic feedback for players post performance. Other coaches feel that they have to detach themselves from players to keep their respect. They feel they have to keep some kind of artificial form of distance. So they choose not to engage with them. They choose to ignore rather than connect with players.

Open lines of communication help your players form a team. Feedback promotes teaming. Here are some guidelines to improve your feedback to individuals.

Be Specific

A simple message of praise or criticism is not enough. It is important to get specific about a component of a player's game. Providing feedback on the actual 'doing' rather than just the more general "things are going great" or "things aren't so good" form of feedback is useful.

What are your players doing differently? What are they more successful at as compared to previous games or training sessions? What specifically can they do to improve an area of their game?

Being specific on instruction not only helps players become a student of *the* game but also a student of *their* game. It not only helps them develop quicker but it also helps them feel valued. It shows them you are paying attention.

Coaches should strive to develop solution focused communication rather than problem focused. How to improve not just what to improve!

Make it Personal

One of the quickest ways to break a feeling of team is to present feedback to an individual comparing him to a team mate. Such feedback can cause a surge in anxiety. A player will feel an unnecessary sense of competition and a sense of 'I am being judged.' When using a comparison pick a player from another team and word your feedback carefully.

"Have you noticed how X does this? You have other attributes that would complement what he does. If you brought that skill into your game it will improve your soccer in a big way."

Goal Oriented

Striving to deliver feedback in relation to a player's goals helps manage motivation. Research has frequently shown that feedback is most effective when it addresses a learner's advancement towards a goal, rather than less meaningful aspects of performance.

In soccer, providing feedback related to a player's training script is useful for a player as it helps him monitor where he is in relation to end goals. If a part of a player's training script is linked with improved positioning in defensive areas and you notice him out of position several times during a training session then feedback straightaway is important. Immediate correction will help this player to adjust accordingly and learn. It helps the player keep the script at the front of his mind.

Don't think that this has little to do with cohesion. Individual feedback buys trust. It commits players to your process. Provided you offer this feedback to all players - it works.

Team Power Plan

You now have individual players willing to team. They are on your side. Provided you continue to care, to take the blame, and to give consistent feedback you'll continue to build trust and they'll stay loyal. Now it's time to start tightening that invisible rope around your players that locks them together and delivers feelings of loyalty amongst themselves.

To do so you need to develop that sense of togetherness.

- *"We are all in this together"*
- *"We know what we want"*
- *"We know how we are going to get there"*

Your players don't have to be best friends. They don't have to have personalities that blend seamlessly. They don't have to have a will to have beers with each other or, if they're younger, to want to visit each other at their respective homes. It is impossible to mould a team through social cohesion alone.

On the other hand having a sense of task cohesion is vital. You must work your backside off for it. You must exercise your imagination to develop ways to improve it. What do I mean by task cohesion? I mean the degree to which the group of players you have, works together towards an agreed upon set of goals and objectives. Sport psychology research has demonstrated that task cohesion is more powerful than social cohesion with relation to outcomes, such as results. Getting your team rallied around the objectives of your club has more impact on the feeling of togetherness than taking your group on an activity outing.

When I am engaged in team building I help coaches draw up what I call a Power Plan. This is a catchy phrase I use instead of the usual 'mission statement' and 'group goal setting'. I want this process to be fun and exciting. I want players to draw on possibilities. I want them to exercise their imagination and envision the future of the team. I want them to begin with the end in mind. I want them to express the important actions that will take them there. And I want them to immerse themselves in the attitudes that back up the actions they believe to be essential for team success.

Ambition

What does your team want to achieve? What is their dream? What is their goal?

I tire of hearing the word 'goal' but the word 'ambition' doesn't bore me. It excites me. It acts as a catalyst for feelings of want and will, for feelings of desire and determination.

I want my teams to have an ambition, an outcome so exciting it supercharges their bodies and minds. I want this to be specific and measurable and I want it to be attainable but stretched. I want the team to come up with it. I want them to take ownership of the outcome they desire.

What that outcome is will depend on the age group and level you coach at. I think it's important to challenge the minds of young soccer players so why not try this exercise with players as young as 10? You could ask them to get themselves into groups and draw the ambition they have as a team for the season. With younger players, winning is far less important than skill development, so you could steer them towards other more skill-based outcomes. There are no hard and fast rules for young players – just make it fun and avoid making the ambition about winning.

Even at the professional clubs I work with I try to help players steer clear of winning as ambition. Last season a team I worked with set themselves a goal of accumulating 101 points over the course of the league competition. They knew that such a points tally would mean automatic promotion into the league above. They knew it was a stretched target but believed if they trained hard, in the right way, and teamed together, they could achieve their ambition.

Once an ambition is selected write it down and spread it amongst your players. Ask them to put it in a prominent position – on their fridge, by their beds or in their kit bags. When they think of soccer they should be thinking of the ambition their team has.

A great coach helps players get excited about their collective ambition. They help set the vision and steer the path

Assets

Just as I ask individuals to re-live their best games and their strengths every day, so I like teams to do the same.

This is a powerful idea. A group of players spotting strengths mediates group confidence. It supports the notion of ambition. It lends towards attitude and action. As leader, taking these assets and making them big and bold and bright and keeping them at the forefront of the players' minds can help you throughout the season. Following a defeat you can return to assets, and following conflict you can return to assets.

- *What 3 things as a team are we strong at?*
- *Last season what were our 3 best performances?*
- *What does our best look like? What does our best feel like?*

Work with these questions. Help your players resonate on the answers by asking them to think in-depth.

Write a short synopsis of their answers. Email it to them. Make a poster that displays strengths – show them off to the world. Remind your players of these assets before every training session. Repeat them after training. Ask them to take five minutes every night to picture them. Reinforce them after victory and after defeat. Build your player's literacy of their performance strengths by immersing them in their special moments. Keep them close to your lips. Keep them stuck on their minds.

Attitudes and Actions

The next step involves building on these assets. It's important to take strengths, and times of success, and use them to create a blueprint of the attitudes and actions your group of players require to meet their ambition.

- *We will show up ten minutes early for training and be on the pitch 10 minutes before we have to be*
- *We will practice one skill a week individually*
- *We will commit to visualising our dream game five minutes a day*
- *We will support each other through our voices*
- *There will be only words of encouragement following a defeat*
- *As individuals we will listen with open minds to comments and corrections*
- *As substitutes or squad players we will support the first team*
- *We will commit to our match script*
- *We will energise each other when we go a goal down*

There are hundreds of mini attitudes and actions you can put into your Power Plan. They can denote simple behaviours that aid your players to focus as individuals, or they can relate to attitudes that help your players' noses point in the same direction.

Have a group session and get down 10-20 key attitudes and actions. Like your group's assets - get them down in writing. Put them on a poster. Get your team to sign their names on the poster to show individual commitment to the group norms they've set.

These are their rules. Help them abide by them. They have set their ambition. They have labelled their assets. They have disciplined their minds to enacting the attitudes and actions they have set themselves.

You have their trust as individuals and now they are developing into a team. The last chapter will help them fly.

12

The Pelican Mindset

The travelling Dutchman carries with him a decade of unrelenting and unsurpassed harmony – his teams synchronized in mind and body. A coach's coach and a 'go-to' guy, the world over, for turnaround or progression.

His remarkable journey East just after the Millennium, a re-introduction of Total Football in his native homeland, his Kangaroos close to jumping the Italian defensive wall, and his influence on the re-emergence of the Russian soccer machine are some of the extraordinary highlights from his CV.

A mid-career blip with the Dutch National team, Real Madrid and Real Betis perhaps fired up Guus Hiddink – or perhaps it relaxed him. Whatever the effect of the discord from the mid to late nineties - since the year 2000 he has found success in every coaching role he's taken on.

The Hiddink Harmony

In 2000, Hiddink took charge of the South Korean National team. The hosts of the 2002 World Cup offered him a chance to shine on the international stage. He would light a beacon that burned bright.

He sculpted a team that was more European than Asian in attitude. Subservience and politeness gave way to personal confidence and performance toughness. In tactical preparation Hiddink adapted what he knew. His brand of Dutch Total Football couldn't be executed by the type of footballers he was going to play against the rest of the world. So he reworked the system. After noting that the team contained players who were physically strong he chose to employ a 3-4-3. The midfield would have flying wingers and a more traditional mix of one attacking, and one defending. For a year he trained them. He drilled them to take on the world's greatest. His reward was a semi final, a fourth place finish, and a cherished spot in the hearts of the South Korean public.

Success in his homeland was to follow as he guided PSV to three League titles in four years and a Champions League semi final – results that demonstrated his ability to adapt straight back to Total Football. A key to his success in Eindhoven was allowing striker Mateja Kezman to play in his own style. While Hiddink didn't shape the team around Kezman he allowed him the freedom to play his natural game. Kezman rewarded Hiddink with 121 goals in 140 games.

Hiddink moved on to managing two national teams in Australia and Russia. He tightened up an Australian defence to help the Socceroos qualify for the World Cup for the first time since 1974. They narrowly lost to Italy in the second round as a result of a dubious penalty decision. And he became Russia's first ever foreign head coach. He helped them progress to the Euro 2008 semi finals with an impressive win over his home country, the Netherlands.

Guus Hiddink is one of the world's best football coaches because he has shown extraordinary capability in creating teams that can win. He accepts the talent he has and he builds a powerful unit that incorporates the specific players that are given to him. He helps his teams fly in formation.

Coaches who can develop a team can develop results

The Pelican Mindset

The pelican's wings beat together as they fly in formation. It helps them soar. It helps them travel the long migration trail without fear of tiring. Their energy expenditure is reduced. In concert, their flying is more efficient.

In concert your players compete with more efficiency.

What science has taught us is that flocks of geese and pelicans fly in V-shaped formations to reduce drag and save energy on long journeys. A study of great white pelicans found that birds flying in formation use up to a fifth less energy than those flying solo. A research team from France recently solved the puzzle as to why birds fly in formation by measuring the heart rates of eight pelicans as they flew in a V formation over Senegal. Their heart beats were compared with the wing beats and flight patterns they displayed. What the researchers found was extraordinary. When flying alone, pelicans beat their wings more frequently than birds flying in formation. It is more tiring for pelicans and geese to fly alone. They may not reach their destination. They may not get home.

As individuals your team may not reach the chosen destination. A team working in unison on the pitch is a product of individuals successfully executing not only the responsibilities they have within their roles, but also the responsibilities they have for their team. This is why, as coach, you must help your players have team targets. You must help them develop the Pelican Mindset.

I understand and appreciate team building activities. Getting members of your team to do an external activity that is fun and sociable and brings players together is useful. Equally, having them complete assault courses and other guided learning group activities can help tighten that invisible rope that binds them. A touch of social cohesion goes a long way to developing combined effort when it counts.

But I'm a great believer that most team building is done in the context specific environment – namely, on the pitch. The work you do on pattern and shape builds your team. The training practices you do with small sided games build your team. The 'piggy in the middle' drill your players enjoy and the passing exercises they do build your team.

As your players train they increase understanding. A nod here, a gesture there – they learn about each other. They learn how another player likes to move, when a player will take a gamble, or risk, and what a player prefers to do in and around the box.

I once worked with a player who had stopped driving for a little time. He was offered lifts into training by a teammate who played in a position close to him. They spent much of their time talking about their philosophies of play and how they saw the game come match day. After a few weeks of this casual car chat both players noticed a difference in their understanding on the pitch. They played cohesively. To some extent they knew what the other was thinking as the game unfolded.

This is real team building. Teaming with performance in mind. As coach it is important to help players play from the same team sheet. They need a common performance language.

Winning teams refuse to be distracted.
They have their targets and they work together, like
crazy, to reach them

A Script for a Team

We will play with loud voices

We will compete with incredible non-stop intensity

The players have two simple instructions – two simple instructions that will help them team. Firstly, they will be vocal and loud. If they go a goal down, they will be loud. They will support each other. If the referee makes a decision they don't like, they will be vocal. They will keep each other focused by reminding others about their team script. They will keep searching for an equaliser by sticking to their team script.

Secondly, the team will show incredible intensity. They will be energetic, alert, alive and lively. This is their pledge as team members. This is their collective goal. This is their vision for the game. They will be non-stop. If they go a goal up, they will demonstrate incredible non-stop intensity. If momentum is piling on them they will show incredible non-stop intensity.

This is their team script. Nothing and no-one will take them away from this. Nothing and no-one! They will live their team script from two hours prior to kick off. They will maintain it together through warm up. They will drive each other on with shared voice and vision, shared thought, and shared mindset. As kick off approaches they will remind each other of their team scripts:

We will play with loud voices

We will compete with incredible non-stop intensity

At kick off - they go. They execute the team script together no matter what. Nothing and no-one moves them from the script. Nothing and no-one.

- *They go a goal down – team script*
- *They go a goal up – team script*
- *The referee blows for a free kick against them – team script*
- *Half time approaching – team script*
- *Fans on their back – team script*
- *Second half first 10 minutes – team script*
- *They equalise – team script*

Nothing and no-one takes them away from their team script. They work together. They work in harmony.

Togetherness requires a common purpose – a series of mini targets that players can buy into

Scripting the Team

All my individual players have a match script. This gives them something to focus on, and to hold onto, in times of need. I want teams to have a script as well. I want a group of players to have a couple of team targets. I want them to play from the same mindset – from a shared mental template.

Chapter 12

Just like an individual match script the team script must revolve around three specific areas:

- *Plays in the script must be controllable*
- *Plays in the script must relate to mastery*
- *Plays in the script must be towards what we want*

To keep plays in the team script controllable make sure they revolve around *your* players, not the oppositions. Also, make sure they are related to the processes of play. For example, neither result nor outcome are controllable factors related to the game. Stick to mastery – the key responsibilities that make up the roles within the team. And make sure any plays are expressed in a positive way – striving not to lose doesn't inspire confidence; motivate players in the right way or help them play front foot football.

Let's look at some other examples of plays you can have in your team script:

- *Press for 5 seconds when we lose the ball, then relax*
- *On our toes at all times*
- *Non-stop high energy*
- *Vocal in set pieces – get organised*
- *Play with pace*
- *Only positive, upbeat communication at all times*
- *Stay in control no matter what*
- *Build from the back*
- *Constant movement – look for spaces*

Of course your team script will involve the tactical side of the game. You will be the best judge of what those plays will be, but make sure you make them controllable. They must be about 'us' and not the opposition.

The team script gives you something to come back to at half time. It is a talking point in coaching sessions and the plays should be worked on and reinforced in training. The plays should be plastered across the walls of the team changing room. They should be emailed or texted to players so that they are immersed in their wording.

They are about 'us'. They are what 'we' do. You need to stereotype them.

*Script the individual, script the team –
have players who are target oriented, then help them
play with freedom*

Building Greater Ownership - Stereotyping

*'We' play hard until the end. 'We' play with intensity. 'We' focus until the very
last kick of the game.*

Research evidence over a number of years has discovered the power of
stereotyping. It has been shown that, to some extent, the roots of poor
performance lie in preconceptions. For example, women who have been led to
believe that they generally do worse than men at mathematics, will perform less
well in a maths test as a result. On the flip side researchers have shown that
stereotypes can act positively to boost performance. For example, research has
shown that Asian women do better on maths tests if they identify themselves as
Asian rather than as women.

This is relevant to soccer. The coach who can build a positive stereotype around
his team is one who can build a robust team. An invisible force field! To a greater
extent this is what Sir Alex Ferguson, Jose Mourinho and Arsene Wenger have
been so good at over the years in British football:

*"This is about us. We are together. Other teams want to beat us because we are
the best. Results show that and we all know it. They are against us. They don't
like us. Everyone wants us to lose. It's us verses the world."*

You can use your team scripts to work on stereotyping your team. "We are the
best" is an admirable message to give your players, but the landscape is more
complicated than this simple sentence. Stereotyping should revolve around the
commitment of the group as well as its identity. "This is what we do" rather than
just "This is who we are".

"This is what we do" includes the plays in the team script. As coach you should
help players commit to these plays in the script and help them to identify
themselves by their processes.

Before his retirement Sir Alex Ferguson's team were notorious for scoring goals
in extra time. It was a period of the match called 'Fergie time' – a name given
due to many people claiming that the referees at Old Trafford gave additional
time for Manchester United to grab a late winner or snatch a draw from the jaws
of defeat. Whether true or not the players still had to score (the reality is that it

was additional time for the opposition to score as well). To my mind Ferguson was brilliant at stereotyping the mental skills of focus and concentration at Manchester United. He often referred to these vital mental qualities and I firmly believe that "We stay switched on for the *whole* game" was a stereotype he created at United. It helped them focus to the final whistle. It helped them play hard to the end.

Your Team

Sir Alex Ferguson, Jose Mourinho, Arsene Wenger, Guus Hiddink, Jurgen Klopp, Pep Guardiola and all the great coaches the world over are successful because they have the knack, the ability, to get great players to share their vision and fight like crazy to reach the pinnacle of this inner picture. They are strong willed, perhaps bloody minded at times. But, by and large, their players fight for them because they know they receive the very best coaching the game has to offer. They know they will be taken care of. They know they will be looked after. Your players will fight for you too, if you get good enough.

Love to lead your players. Make them feel great. Help them feel important. Take your players on a journey. If they are young then immerse them in developing the skills they need. If they are adult players still take time to develop them as individuals but place an emphasis on teaming them. This isn't necessarily done down the pub or at the bowling alley. It's done on your favourite terrain – the pitch. It's done in every training session and it's done by giving them the script that emphasises "This is how we play" and "This is what we do".

Coaching is impossible to perfect. It is the toughest of all professions and the toughest of all hobbies. You deal with people's dreams. You deal with people's failures. You trade in their passions. But the better you get, the more fun you have. And that is all you can ask of yourself when you take to the pitch.

Driving Your Culture of Cohesion

SHOW Leadership

S - A soccer coach must be a servant to his or her players and people.
H - A soccer coach must be an accomplished host.
O - A soccer coach must lead through optimism.
W - A soccer coach must be wilful of heart and of mind.

Reflect through different lenses

As a soccer leader you need to develop the capacity to reflect. Reflection helps you gain a genuine understanding of yourself and others within your club. It can be uncomfortable, but in its absence there is a constant risk of poor decisions.

Think the 'me' before the 'we'

There is no I in team but there is in win. To build a team you must get individual players onside first. You don't have to be their best friend but they must trust and respect your ability to coach them. They must want to fight for you.

Develop a power plan

Ambitions are exciting and powerful. Find out what your players' collective ambition is. Search for the assets in your team – things that make the ambition possible. Then explore the attitudes and actions you need to execute together, every day.

Build the pelican mindset

Help your team to fly in formation by introducing them to the pelican mindset. Your players need to work together – in concert they compete with more efficiency. Social cohesion is useful, but real bonding is done on the training pitch.

Script your team

Just as your individual players should have a match script, so your players should have a team script. Insist your players have a couple of team targets. Help them to play from the same mindset – from a shared mental template.

Stereotype your team

The best coaches in the world speak in terms of 'us' and 'we'. Use the plays in your team script to build a sense of "This is what we do in this team". Stereotype your team positively and enjoy win after win after win.

Conclusion
A Culture of Success

Coaching Her

She is ready for this game. She's ready because you've helped her. Your words resonate in her mind and the extra coaching you've done with her over the past few weeks has settled her soccer brain.

She is a product of your culture of creativity.

She is a free footballer. She looks up and checks her shoulders. She sees her teammates clearly. She sees the positions of the opposition players. She has clarity and an awareness of the pitch around her.

She is a product of your culture of confidence.

She skips inside the challenge of one player and releases the ball to a teammate in space. With confidence, with desire, and with determination, she runs into space, checks her body shape to receive the ball on the half turn and demands the ball back. She gets it and takes on the centre back. She rounds the defender and takes a shot which flashes past the post. She's missed again, the 5th time that half. But she won't let it affect her. She skips back to the half way line and takes up her position again.

She is a product of your culture of commitment.

She has feedback for her teammates at half time. The ordinary player would baulk at the audacity, but these are *your* players. They are extraordinary. They are playing together. They are a collection of individuals playing as one.

She is a product of your culture of cohesion.

Coaching Him

He loves your training sessions. There is always something new for him to try. He loves the fact that you have helped him become fitter, stronger and more combative. This is down to the new fitness regime you have introduced to his team.

He is a product of your culture of creativity.

He shadows past his teammates. He is loose, he is free, he is confident. He expresses himself – making runs – on his toes, alert, alive and lively. Shackles off – he knows he can take risks. He knows he can make mistakes without repercussions.

He is a product of your culture of confidence.

He has a training script that he fixes his attention on. He's improving the small things in his game – the fine details. He now knows the art of intentional practice and he intends to use its science. He intends to realise a game he'd never dreamt of.

He is a product of your culture of commitment.

After the training session he comes to you – he knows he can speak and you will listen. He tells you about a few challenges he is facing with his teammates. You have a few suggestions as to how he can improve his relationship with them. You promise you will help him feel more a part of the team.

He is a product of your culture of cohesion.

Coaching Them

They are ready for the cup final. They should be – they have been exposed to video analysis for the first time ever. They have seen themselves play – as individuals and as a team. They have the evidence of their performances on camera – no more guesswork.

They are a product of your culture of creativity

They have trained to the beat of confidence. They have been reminded of their best game together. They have imagined their dream game as individuals and as a team. Their positive pictures are lodged firmly in their minds – they have been doing these mental exercises in every training session for many months.

They are a product of your culture of confidence.

They know what can go wrong in a match. They don't dwell on these negative images but such inner pictures allow them to appreciate plan B. They understand this notion. They know that not everything can go perfectly on match day and they appreciate that having a set of solutions will help them deal with any adversity that may strike.

They are a product of your culture of commitment.

At the end of the training session they are huddled together. They have a match the next day so they run over their team script. A game against top of the table opponents requires plays in their script that help them compete with intensity. They write this down. They will work hard together. They will work hard for each other.

They are a product of your culture of cohesion.

Coaching Culture

What does success look like to you? A cup win? A league championship? A couple of players making it pro? A bunch of 10 year olds loving every second of every minute of their sessions with you? Being the best leader you can be?

There are hundreds of thousands of soccer coaches the world over. Each of you will have a different set of goals for your players. But each of you can prosper if you work on building and establishing the four cultures described in this book. Your players will improve, they will win, and they will have fun doing it.

Conclusion

Build a culture of creativity. Learn all you can and become a student of the game. Find the 1% nudges and introduce your players to something new in your training sessions – perhaps every session. Grow your talent, but remember ability comes in different forms – appreciate what they *do* have.

Build a culture of confidence. Give them the belief they need to build skill quickly and effectively. Open your self-belief tool kit regularly – give them the pleasure of exploring strengths, best moments, and dream games. Within personal recollection and human imagination lie exciting internal pictures that expand the feeling of confidence, of high performance. And let them experience the feeling of confidence as they train. Immerse them in this feeling – let this physiological snapshot of positive emotion become habit and pattern – perhaps addiction.

Build a culture of commitment. Help them dance their feet when pressure bears down and when mistakes can burden their focus. Help them prepare thoroughly for the game at hand. Ask them to think of the worst and watch as they continue to play unencumbered in spite of best laid plans gone wrong. And help them walk their confident talk by introducing them to intentional practice. This new, improved training mindset will absorb their brain in a deeper, richer form of learning. It is intentional practice, the art of training with complete focus, away from comfort zone and with a purpose that separates soccer players.

Build a culture of cohesion. Be the leader they need you to be – SHOW leadership at all times. Be the detailed servant, be the captivating host, be the optimist and display will – full of desire and determination. Create the 'we' but appreciate the 'me' in 'we'. And lay down the process of performance for your team. Together they will fight.

You, the coach, feed your coaching culture just as it feeds your improvement as a teacher. Monitor your own performance everyday and find the shifts and the nudges to improve your processes and your systems regularly. Great coaches demand more from themselves than they do from their players.

No matter what age, no matter what gender, no matter what level, no matter what country - your coaching culture will drive players' soccer mindsets, their soccer technique, their physicality, and their application of the tactical plays you set out for them. Whether your club is all-inclusive, or whether it is elite, forming your coaching culture will drive players' characters. It will drive their development. It will drive their performances. It will drive their Soccer Brain.

Graduation: Life Lessons of a Professional Footballer by Richard Lee

The 2010/11 season will go down as a memorable one for Goalkeeper Richard Lee. Cup wins, penalty saves, hypnotherapy and injury would follow, but these things only tell a small part of the tale. Filled with anecdotes, insights, humour and honesty - Graduation uncovers Richard's campaign to take back the number one spot, save a lot of penalties, and overcome new challenges. What we see is a transformation - beautifully encapsulated in this extraordinary season.

"Whatever level you have played the beautiful game and whether a goalkeeper or outfield player, you will connect with this book. Richard's honesty exposes the fragility in us all, he gives an honest insight into dimensions of a footballer's life that are often kept a secret and in doing so offers worthy advice on how to overcome any hurdle. A great read." **Ben Foster, Goalkeeper, West Bromwich Albion.**

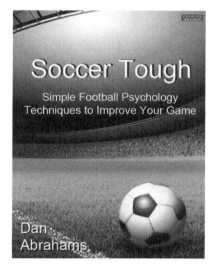

Soccer Tough by Dan Abrahams

"Take a minute to slip into the mind of one of the world's greatest soccer players and imagine a stadium around you. Picture a performance under the lights and mentally play the perfect game."

Technique, speed and tactical execution are crucial components of winning soccer, but it is mental toughness that marks out the very best players – the ability to play when pressure is highest, the opposition is strongest, and fear is greatest. Top players and coaches understand the importance of sport psychology in soccer but how do you actually train your mind to become the best player you can be?

Soccer Tough demystifies this crucial side of the game and offers practical techniques that will enable soccer players of all abilities to actively develop focus, energy, and confidence. Soccer Tough will help banish the fear, mistakes, and mental limits that holds players back.

Scientific Approaches to Goalkeeping in Football: A practical perspective on the most unique position in sport
by Andy Elleray

Do you coach goalkeepers and want to help them realise their fullest potential? Are you a goalkeeper looking to reach the top of your game? Then search no further and dive into this dedicated goalkeeping resource. Written by goalkeeping guru Andy Elleray this book offers a fresh and innovative approach to goalkeeping in football. With a particular emphasis on the development of young goalkeepers, it sheds light on training, player development, match performances, and player analysis. Utilising his own experiences Andy shows the reader various approaches, systems and exercises that will enable goalkeepers to train effectively and appropriately to bring out the very best in them.

Small Time: A Life in the Football Wilderness by Justin Bryant

In 1988, 23-year-old American goalkeeper Justin Bryant thought a glorious career in professional football awaited him. He had just saved two penalties for his American club - the Orlando Lions - against Scotland's Dunfermline Athletic, to help claim the first piece of silverware in their history. He was young, strong, healthy, and confident.

Small Time is the story of a life spent mostly in the backwaters of the game. As Justin negotiated the Non-League pitches of the Vauxhall-Opel League, and the many failed professional leagues of the U.S. in the 1980s and 90s - Football, he learned, is 95% blood, sweat, and tears; but if you love it enough, the other 5% makes up for it.

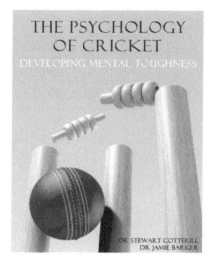

The Psychology of Cricket: Developing Mental Toughness [Cricket Academy Series]
by Dr. Stewart Cotterill and Dr. Jamie Barker

The mental side of cricket is what separates the best players from the rest. Technical, tactical, and physical preparation are important for top class performances but it is often what happens inside a player's mind that is the difference between success and failure. Whether batting, bowling, or fielding, a player's psychological strength has been identified by coaches, players, and commentators as a critical ingredient for winning cricket matches.

The Psychology of Cricket teaches individuals to develop mental toughness by using mental skills which can be used in both practice and match situations. The book also provides expert advice on understanding the important ingredients of successful teams and leaders.

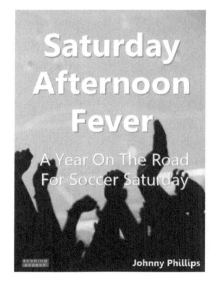

Saturday Afternoon Fever: A Year On The Road For Soccer Saturday
by Johnny Phillips

You might already know Johnny Phillips. He is a football reporter for Sky Sports' Soccer Saturday programme and a man who gets beamed into the homes of fans across the country every weekend.

For the 2012/13 season, Johnny decided to do something different. He wanted to look beneath the veneer of household-name superstars and back-page glamour to chronicle a different side to our national sport. As Johnny travelled the country, he found a game that he loved even more, where the unheralded stars were not only driven by a desire to succeed but also told stories of bravery and overcoming adversity, often to be plucked from obscurity into the spotlight… and sometimes dropped back into obscurity again. Football stories that rarely see the limelight but have a value all fans can readily identify with.

CPSIA information can be obtained at www.ICGtesting.com
Printed in the USA
LVOW03s1514050914

402654LV00008B/275/P

9 781909 125049